Glazing Techniques

Joaquim Chavarria

WATSON-GUPTILL PUBLICATIONS/NEW YORK

Ceramics Class: Glazing Techniques
Original Spanish title:
   Aula de cerámica: Esmaltes
Editorial director: María Fernanda Canal
Text and exercises: Joaquim Chavarria
Graphic Design: Carlos Bonet
Diagrams: SET. Seveis Editorials i Técnics
Dummy: Pedro González
Photography: Nos & Soto
Archive research: Mª Carmen Ramos
Translation: Mark Lodge

First published in the United States in 1999 by Watson-Guptill
Publications, a division of BPI Communications, Inc.
1515 Broadway, New York, N.Y. 10036

Copyright © 1998 Parramón Ediciones, S.A.
Gran Via de les Corts Catalanes, 322-324
08004 Barcelona, Spain

Library of Congress Catalog Card Number: 98-83066
ISBN 0-8230-0592-5

Manufactured in Spain

1 2 3 4 5 6 / 04 03 02 01 00 99

CONTENTS

Introduction	5
Glaze Materials	6
Basic Coloring Oxides	8
Glaze Calculation	10
Types of Glazes	12
Glazing Equipment	13
Preparing Glazes	14
Glazes and Commercially Sold Ceramic Pigments	16
Kilns and Accessories	18
Packing the Kiln and Firing	22
Temperature and Color Considerations in Firing	24
Glazing with the Dipping Method	26
Glazing with the Pouring Method	28
Glazing with a Brush	30
Glazing with a Spraygun	32
Testing for and Correcting Glazing Defects	34

Low- and Medium-Temperature Glazes	38
High- and Very-High-Temperature Glazes	40
Crystalline Glazes	42
Raku	44
Salt Glazes	46
Ash Glazes	48
Crackle Glazes	50
Scotch Topaz Glazes	53
Reduction Firing	54
Celadon Glazes	54
Oxblood Glazes	56
Single-Firing	58
Lusters	60
Preparing Frits	62
Glossary	64

INTRODUCTION

Many years ago, when I was just beginning my career in ceramics, I heard someone at a conference declare, "In ceramics, the wheel is to shape what the kiln is to glazing." With time, I began to understand what this meant. Glazing is the final step in creating a ceramic piece, and on some level the most important. It can either give it the desired finish or ruin the work altogether. It is thus essential to understand the characteristics of the glaze components, how to mix and apply them, and how to fire the piece correctly.

At first, glazing may seem complicated and it may take a while to get the knack. But the information in this book is simple and thorough, and requires only basic technical knowledge. Only a few formulas are needed, but they must be sound, allowing the glaze to melt within the adequate firing temperatures for good results. In general, there are several basic formulas that can be varied by changing and combining materials and percentages, and adding coloring oxides in an infinite number of combinations.

This book explains the series of processes involved in glazing, beginning with the materials necessary to prepare a glaze, the methods of mixing these materials, and an explanation of different types of glazes and how to prepare them. After this is a discussion of kilns and firing techniques, different methods of applying glazes, and how to identify possible defects and correct them. Following these basics of working with glazes is an analysis of the most well known among the various glaze types, with a general explanation of each to help you learn how to combine them into more complex, personalized versions.

Some of the objects seen here require a preliminary glazing, which should be prepared carefully with precisely mixed doses before firing. Many of the pieces shown have been created solely to illustrate what is being explained. Others were made in previous years but serve as good examples. Practice and experiment with the formulas when preparing and firing sample pieces to see what works best for you.

Testing glazes is very important. Whether the results are good or bad, they can help us better understand different glaze properties if we know how to analyze them. Researching new glazes can teach us how they will react to one another. With practice, once you have planned a piece you should be able to decide what method will produce good technical and aesthetic results.

If you are already experienced in various hand-building techniques and are capable of throwing symmetrical pieces, this is the "test of fire," since, after all our efforts, it is the firing that will give the piece its definitive finish. The kiln can't work miracles; on the contrary, it does exactly what we ask of it. We must therefore learn to control it.

Hopefully beginners will have few difficulties, but bad experiences needn't be considered as such, since they offer learning opportunities. Do not lose heart. Study, practice, and will power are the ingredients necessary to achieve the best results. In addition to talent, imagination, and artistic sensibility, the ceramist must gain solid technical knowledge of the field. To all those about to take up ceramics and to all those already on their way, my best wishes.

Joaquim-Manuel Chavarria Climent

GLAZE MATERIALS

Glazes appear to date back to about 2000 to 1000 B.C, when potters from Mesopotamia developed a vitreous (transparent) glaze to cover bricks and, later, pottery. After this, bricks and wall tiles were decorated with lead-based glazes, which turned an opaque white with the addition of tin oxide. Subsequently, natural glazes were discovered, such as the ash glaze developed by Chinese potters.

Basically, ceramic glazes are prepared by mixing selected materials in the correct proportions, along with water. They are then applied over the entire surface of raw or bisque-fired ceramic pieces. When fired, the mixture melts into a vitreous paste that adheres to the piece.

At least two basic elements are necessary in a glaze mixture: a vitrifying agent, such as silica, and a melting agent, such as lead or borax. The combination of these two agents produces a transparent, shiny substance. Silica, generally the principal ingredient, has a very high melting point (1700°C; 3092°F).

In glazes with low melting points, various materials can be used as fluxing agents: lead composites (minium, litharge, galena, and lead carbonate) and alkaline composites (borax, boric acid, sodium carbonate, and colemanite). In glazes with high melting points, feldspar is the main ingredient.

Materials

Glazing materials are natural or manufactured products normally used for industrial purposes, and which the potter uses in preparing ceramic mixtures and glazes. Following are some of those most commonly used in preparing glazes.

Alumina. Al_2O_3. Aluminum oxide, molecular weight (Mw) 102. It is added to glaze mixtures in a very small proportion. It heightens viscosity, hardness, and resistance to pressure, and it prevents dripping. It is a neutral oxide, located in the central column of the Seger formula (see pages 10–11). It produces matte surfaces when added in elevated percentages, and can even prevent the glaze from fusing. It is insoluble and can be found as alumina hydrate, $Al_2(OH)_6$, Mw 156.

Antimony oxide. Sb_3O_3, Mw 291. In a lead base it produces yellows, and in an alkaline base, whites, in both cases opaque. It can cause lead-based glazes to bubble. It is opacifying and highly toxic.

Barium carbonate. $BaCO_3$, Mw 197.3. It is used in combination with other fluxes. In low-temperature glazes, it is refractory and should therefore be used in small proportions. It produces matte finishes. It is a very active flux in high-temperature glazes, acting as an opacifier. It is insoluble and toxic.

Bone ash or calcium phosphate. $Ca_3(PO_4)_2$, Mw 310, specific gravity 103. It is obtained by calcinating animal bones. It acts as an opacifier in glazes that fire at high temperatures. It is also used in clay mixtures called bone porcelain, in which it acts as a fluxing agent as well as an opacifier.

Boric oxide. B_2O_3, Mw 69.6. Insoluble, it is used both raw and fritted. It should be used shortly after it is prepared. The borax also supplies boric oxide. The calcinated or anhydrous variety should be used, $Na_2O. 2B_2O_3$, Mw

202. It is nontoxic. It does not have the characteristics of lead-based glazes. Colemanite is one of the insoluble borides that supplies glazes with boron.

Calcium carbonate. $CaCO_3$, Mw 100. It adds calcium oxide to glazes. Also called whiting, it can make low-temperature glazes bubble, and thus the best thing is to calcinate it, which transforms it into calcium oxide (CaO), Mw 56; this should be taken into account when calculating the formula for the glaze. It is insoluble and fluxes at high temperatures, and can also act as an opacifier. Other minerals that contain calcium are Wollastonite, $CaSiO_3$, Mw 116; Fluorspar, CaF_2, Mw 78; and Dolomite, $CaCO_3.MgCO_3$, Mw 184.

Colemanite. $2CaO.3B_2O_3.5H_2O$, Mw 412, specific gravity 206. Hydrous calcium borate. It provides boron. It is insoluble. To avoid causing bubbles in the glaze, it should be calcinated at 820°C (1508°F).

Cryolite. Na_3AlF_6, Mw 210. Sodium aluminum fluoride. It is used as a source of insoluble sodium oxide. The fluoride can cause the glaze to bubble during firing.

Dolomite. $CaCO_3.MgCO_3$, Mw 184. Calcium carbonate and magnesium. It is made from calcium oxide and mag-

A. Zirconium oxide. B. Petalite.
C. Lithium carbonate.
D. Minium. E. Ilmenite.
F. Borax. G. Litharge.
H. Tricalcium phosphate.
I. Mullite. J. Zinc oxide.

nesium in insoluble form. It is also used to prepare clay body.

Feldspar. Anhydrous aluminum silicate, with sodium and potassium. A basic ingredient in the preparation of clay body and glazes, especially for high-temperature firing, it has an alkaline component (the sodium and potassium), alumina and silica, and sometimes calcium and lithium. It is insoluble.

Feldspar comes in different varieties according to its composition:

Containing potassium or orthoclase: $K_2O.Al_2O_3.6SiO_2$, Mw 556.

Containing sodium or albite: $Na_2O.Al_2O_3.6SiO_2$, Mw 524

Containing calcium or anorthite: $CaO.Al_2O_3.2SiO$, Mw 278.

Containing lithium or spodumene: $LiO_2.Al_2O_3.4SiO_2$, Mw 372.

Containing petalite: $LiO_2.Al_2O_3.8SiO_2$, Mw 612

Fluorspar. CaF_2, Mw 78. Also called calcium fluoride, or fluorite. Used in glazes as an opacifier and a flux, it is a source of calcium and fluoride in insoluble form. It can make glazes bubble if added in a ratio of more than 5 percent.

Galena. PbS, Mw 239. Lead sulfide. It is little used today.

Ilmenite. $TiO_2.FeO$, Mw 152. Ferrous titanite. An impure mineral containing titanium and iron. If applied in a thick layer, it causes the glaze to mottle with black dots.

Lead carbonate. $2PbCO_3$. $Pb(OH)_2$, Mw 775, specific gravity 258. Also known as white lead or ceruse. It adds lead oxide in insoluble form to glazes. It is highly toxic.

Litharge. PbO, Mw 223. Lead monoxide, pale yellow in color. It is used to prepare lead frit and also raw glaze. It is insoluble and toxic.

Lithium carbonate. Li_2CO_3, Mw 74. It introduces lithium into glazes and greatly fluxes at high temperatures. It can take the place of lead at medium temperatures. It favors crystalline glazes, reduces thermal dilation in glazes, and increases their resistance. It is insoluble. Other sources of lithium are Petalite, $Li_2O.Al_2O_3.8SiO_2$, Mw 612; Spodumene, $Li_2O.Al_2O_3.4SiO_2$, Mw 372; and Lepidolite, $(LiNaK)_2.(FOH_2.Al_2O_3.3SiO_2$, Mw 472. The fluoride that lepidolite contains can cause the glaze to bubble during firing.

Magnesium carbonate. $MgCO_3$, Mw 84. It acts as a refractory agent at low temperatures and as a flux at high temperatures. It improves the adhesive capacity of glazes and reduces the fluidity of those that have a tendency to drip. It is volatile and not very soluble, and must be mixed in a dry state with the other components of the glaze.

Minium. Pb_3O_4, Mw 685, specific gravity 228. Lead oxide, bright red in color. It is a basic ingredient in the

A. Calcium carbonate
B. Tin oxide
C. Fluorspar
D. Titanium oxide
E. Potassium dichromate
F. Barium carbonate
G. Talc
H. Wollastonite
I. Cryolite
J. Magnesium carbonate

preparation of raw lead-based glazes, which are fired in an oxidation kiln. It is insoluble and highly toxic.

Potassium carbonate. KCO_3, Mw 138. Provides potassium oxide. It has a very fluxible alkaline base. It is used as a frit. It is deliquescent and soluble.

Quartz. SiO_2. Silicon oxide, Mw 60. It is a basic ingredient in the preparation of clay body and glazes, providing silica. Low-firing glazes contain two-thirds quartz, whereas high-firing ones contain three-fourths.

Rutile. TiO_2. This is titanium oxide in its natural state. It can be impure, sometimes containing iron oxide.

Steatite. $3MgO.4SiO_2.H_2O$, Mw 379, specific gravity 126. Hydrous magnesium silicate, a derivative of talc. It provides magnesium and silica.

Talc. Its formula can vary from $3MgO.4SiO_2.H_2O$, with Mw 379 and * 126, to $4MgO.5SiO_2.H_2O$. Hydrous magnesium silicate. Provides magnesium and silica (like steatite). It should be mixed in a dry state with the other glaze ingredients.

Tin oxide. SnO_2, Mw 151. Stannic oxide, the most effective opacifier. In quantities greater than 5–7 percent, it produces a completely opaque white glaze. It can be added to both raw and fritted glazes. It is insoluble, and its opacifying capacity increases when it is used together with titanium and zinc.

Wollastonite. $CaO.SiO_2$, Mw 116. Calcium metasilicate. It can be used as a source of calcium for glazes. It produces crystals. It also changes the color shade of the glaze and acts as an opacifier.

Zinc oxide. ZnO, Mw 81. It is a very strong flux at high temperatures. It increases the maturation interval of glazes. It can produce crystalline structures in glazes with low alumina content. It is insoluble and can be used as a flux in low-firing glazes as well. It acts as an opacifier when used in combination with titanium. It modifies the colors produced by coloring oxides.

Zirconium oxide. ZrO_2, Mw 123. Can be used as an opacifier in glazes in place of tin, but does not provide the same quality. It is insoluble and, when used in combination with zinc, adds color tones to glazes.

BASIC COLORING OXIDES

Glazes get their color through the addition of metal oxides such as cobalt, copper, chrome, iron, manganese, nickel, vanadium, and other, less common metals. Each oxide produces a characteristic color, which can be modified by other glaze components. Such changes can be caused by the firing temperature or the atmosphere inside the kiln, as well as by additional coloring oxides that can be mixed in. Some oxides (such as cobalt, copper, iron, and manganese) reduce the fluxing temperature of the glaze, while others (such as antimony, chrome, tin, and nickel) increase it.

Antimony. Sb_2O_3, Mw 291.5. Antimony trioxide. It produces yellows when combined with lead-based glazes in a ratio of 1–2 percent. It should be calcinated at 900°C (1641°F) to prevent it from bubbling. In alkaline glazes it produces a white color (4–6 percent). It is not very soluble in water and volatilizes at 1000°C (1802°F) or higher. It is highly toxic.

Cadmium. CdS, Mw 144.4. Cadmium sulfide. Used in low-temperature glazes, it produces reds and oranges when mixed with selenium (Se), and yellows when mixed with sulfur (S).

Chrome. CrO_2, Mw 152. Chromic oxide. Produces greens. When mixed with lead-based glazes, it produces reds at 930–950°C (1706–1742°F) in a ratio of 2.5 percent, and orange at 1.5 percent. When the temperature is raised, it produces hard greens, and when mixed with tin and calcium, light pinks. With zinc and lead bases, it produces browns; with titanium and in alkaline glazes, dark browns are produced. It is insoluble.

Cobalt. CoO, Mw 75. Cobal-

It is important to remember that elevated proportions of coloring oxides will produce black (metallic) colors. In high-temperature glazes, the amount of oxide must be increased, often varying greatly from the amount added to low-temperature ones.

tous oxide. Co$_2$O$_3$, Mw 165.8. Cobaltic oxide. These are blackish in color and are insoluble. Cobalt is the oxide with the highest coloring strength. In low-temperature glazes it produces blues (0.1–1 percent) but must be used in greater percentages in high-temperature glazes. If mixed with zinc, iron, manganese, or titanium it will produce softer blues. It produces calcium carbonate (CoCO$_3$, Mw 119) when calcinated at 1000–1040°C (1802–1904°F), which has a lesser concentration of coloring agent. It is insoluble.

Copper. CuO, Mw 79.5. Cupric oxide. Cu$_2$O, Mw 143. Cuprous oxide. CuCO$_3$, Mw 123.5. Copper carbonate. It produces a green color in lead-based glazes and turquoise in alkaline ones. In a reduction atmosphere, it provides reddish colors (oxblood). Proportions vary from 1.5 to 3 percent for low-temperature glazes; in the high-temperature glazes, they rise to 2.5–5 percent. It is insoluble.

Iron. Fe$_2$O$_3$, Mw 160. Ferric oxide, reddish in color. FeO, Mw 72. Ferrous oxide, grayish black in color. A golden color is produced when it is added in a proportion of 2–3 percent to lead-based glazes.

In alkaline glazes it produces beige, and in a reduction atmosphere and elevated temperatures, grayish green (celadon). Combined with other oxides, such as cobalt, copper, or manganese, it produces black. It is insoluble.

Iron chromate. Fe$_2$O$_3$.Cr$_2$O$_3$, Mw 759.7. It produces brownish and grayish colors.

Lead chromate. PbCrO$_4$, Mw 323. Produces yellow-orange colors in lead-based glazes. It is soluble in hot water.

Manganese. MnO$_2$, Mw 87. Manganese dioxide, blackish in color. It should be calcinated at 1000–1040°C (1802–1904°F). With lead-based glazes, it produces purples, violets, and browns (0.5–2 percent). Pink tones can also be obtained. In higher proportions (10–15 percent), a metallic, iridescent black results. With cobalt, black is obtained. With alkaline fluxes, reddish and purplish tones can be produced. It is insoluble.

Nickel. NiO, Mw 75. Nickelous oxide, greenish gray in color. Ni$_2$O$_3$, Mw 166. Nickelic oxide, gray in color. Alone, it produces grayish greens and greenish blacks. Depending on the flux used and the amount of alumina added, various colors can be obtained: zinc yields blue; barium, coffee brown; magnesium, green. It modifies the color of other oxides. The proportion is 1–3 percent. Browns are obtained at high temperatures. It is insoluble.

Potassium dichromate. K$_2$Cr$_2$O$_7$, Mw 294. Reddish in color, it produces yellows, oranges, reds, and greens. It is soluble and highly toxic.

Uranium. UO$_2$, Mw 270. Uranous oxide. Yellow in color, it produces reds and oranges in lead-based glazes. If the temperature is raised, yellow is obtained.

Vanadium. V$_2$O$_5$, Mw 182. Vanadium pentoxide, yellow-ochre in color. It produces faded shades of yellow and orange in proportions of 2–10 percent. These colors become brighter when combined with tin oxide and titanium. With zirconium (Zr), turquoise is produced; with iron (Fe), ochres; with manganese (Mn), yellowish browns.

A. Vanadium pentoxide
B. Cobalt oxide
C. Chrome oxide
D. Cobalt carbonate
E. Uranous oxide
F. Nickel oxide
G. Copper oxide
H. Antimony oxide
I. Magnesium dioxide
J. Iron chromate
K. Lead chromate
L. Copper carbonate

GLAZE CALCULATION

To calculate a glaze, it is necessary to know the behavior of its component materials. As already explained in the section on materials (see pages 6–7), ceramic glazes are composed of at least two elements, a vitrifying agent and a flux. Refractory components, such as alumina, can be added as well.

To learn how to make a glaze recipe, you will need to know some chemical formulas, know how to read and understand the chemical symbols of the elements, and know their atomic weights.

The task of calculating the formulas and making the recipes is easy if you apply the classification system for glaze oxides created in the nineteenth century by German chemist Herman Seger. Seger divided part of the oxides in glazes into three groups: basic oxides (fluxes), neutral oxides, and acid oxides.

Within the **base oxides** category are the oxides whose chemical formulas are of the type RO/R_2O, where R is the chemical element that combines with oxygen to form an oxide. In this group are the lithium oxides (Li_2O), sodium (Na_2O), potassium (K_2O), calcium (CaO), magnesium (MgO), barium (BaO), zinc (ZnO), strontium (SrO), and lead (PbO).

In the **neutral oxides** category, the formula is R_2O_3. This group includes aluminum oxide (Al_2O_3) and boron oxide (B_2O_3). Boric oxide can act as a base or an acid, with the capacity to partially replace silicon and lower the fluxing temperature practically without altering the glaze. It can also be introduced in insoluble form, such as colemanite or hydrous boracite (calcium and magnesium borate).

The **acid oxides** category has the formula RO_2. Silicon oxide (SiO_2) is part of this group.

The Seger formula is always be presented in three columns in the following manner:

Bases	Neutrals	Acids
RO/R_2O	R_2O_3	RO_2

Once this classification is done, the formula establishes that the oxides are not expressed by weight but as mole or fractions of mole.

Keep the following points in mind:

1. The base oxides (fluxes) of type RO/R_2O are written at the left of the Seger formula and are expressed in mole fractions. It is essential that their sum be 1; that is, that the formula be unitary.

2. The neutral oxides occupy the central part of the Seger formula; the most commonly used is aluminum oxide. The proportion of this oxide can vary from 0.1 to 1.5 molecules and is ideally one-tenth of the molecules in the silicon.

3. The acid oxides column is placed at the right of the Seger formula and can vary from 1.5 to 15 molecules of silicon.

Finally, remember that the RO/RO_2 group consists of fluxes, the R_2O_3 group contains refractory elements, and the RO_2 group consists of the vitrifying agents. Coloring oxides, which are added in small quantities, do not form part of the formula because they do not alter the chemical process.

Following is an example to illustrate these concepts. In the example, there is one molecule of silicon for each half molecule of lead, calcium, and aluminum oxides.

Bases		Neutral		Acids	
PbO	0.5	Al_2O_3	0.5	SiO_2	1
CaO	0.5				

Determining a Unitary Formula from a Recipe

To calculate the formula, we will use a recipe for low-temperature glazes (960°C/1730°F). Let's assume a recipe consisting of:

Litharge 55 parts
Silica   35 parts
Chalk   10 parts

First of all, we must know which oxides each of the ingredients provides to the formula: litharge contains lead oxide (PbO), silica is silicon oxide (SiO_2), and chalk is calcium carbonate ($CaCO_2$). Calculate the molecular weight (Mw):

Litharge Mw = 223
Silica   Mw = 60
Chalk   Mw = 100

If we know the proportion in which each component is present and its molecular weight, then we can calculate the moles by dividing the former by the latter.

Litharge 55 ÷ 223 =
    0.246 moles of PbO
Silica 35 ÷ 60 =
    0.583 moles of SiO_2
Chalk 10 ÷ 100 =
    0.1 moles of CaO

Then we must calculate the unitary formula according to the Seger formula.

Vase, 1980. Thrown stoneware, 31.5 × 10 cm (12 1/2 × 4 in). Feldspathic glaze with 3% titanium dioxide and cobalt carbonate. Firing temperature: 1260°C (2300°F).

Bases		Neutral	Acids	
PbO	0.246	none	SiO_2	0.583
CaO	0.1			

Add up the fractions in the first column, for a total of 0.346. Since this is not equal to a unit, we will have to divide it by itself, and the silica likewise.

PbO	0.246	÷ 0.346 =	0.710
CaO	0.1	÷ 0.346 =	0.289
			= 0.999 @ 1
SiO_2	0.583	÷ 0.346	= 1.68

Thus, the unitary formula for the recipe expressed in moles will look like this:

Bases		Neutral	Acids	
PbO	0.710	—	SiO_2	1.68
CaO	0.289			

Another Example
In order to better comprehend the previous process, let's calculate another formula, this time with the recipe for a high-temperature glaze.

Potassium feldspar $K_2O.Al_2O_3.6SiO_2$ Mw 556

Calcium carbonate $CaCO_3$ Mw 100

Divide the weight of each component by its respective molecular weight:

Potassium feldspar $80 \div 556 = 0.14$
Calcium carbonate $20 \div 100 = 0.2$

Placed according to the Seger formula, they look like this:

Bases		Neutral		Acids
K_2O	0.14	Al_2O_3	0.14	SiO_2 0.14
$CaCO$	0.2			

Given that potassium feldspar has six molecules of silicon, the moles must be multiplied by six: 6 x 0.14 = 0.84

Since the sum of the base group must equal 1, each element in this group is divided by its sum. The same is done for the components in the other groups. The sum of the base oxides is: 0.34.

K_2O $0.1 \div 0.34 = 0.41$
$CaCO_3$ $0.2 \div 0.34 = 0.58$
Al_2O_3 $0.14 \div 0.34 = 0.41$
SiO_2 $0.84 \div 0.34 = 2.47$

The formula looks like this:

Bases		Neutral		Acids
K_2O	0.41	Al_2O_3	0.41	SiO_2 2.47
$CaCO_3$	0.58			

Calculating a Recipe from a Formula

Now let's try the opposite operation: use an empirical formula to calculate the recipe for a low-temperature glaze. We'll use a simple, unitary formula, without neutral oxides:

PbO   0.8   —
SiO_2 1
CaO   0.2

First choose the raw materials with which you will work; for example, minium, calcium carbonate, and silicon. We also know their molecular weights.
PbO   0.8 x 223 = 178.4 parts minium
CaO   0.2 x 100 = 20 parts calcium carbonate

SiO_2 1 x 60   = 60 parts silicon
                                      258.4

To reduce the recipe to decimals, multiply the result of each component by 100 and divide by the total sum:

Minium $178.4 \times 100 \div 258.4 = 69.0$ parts
Calcium carbonate $20 \times 100 \div 258.4 = 7.7$ parts
Silica $60 \times 100 \div 258.4 = 23.3$ parts

The sums obtained express in weight the quantities of each material needed to make the recipe. Having reduced the recipe to decimals, the addition of coloring oxides or other coloring agents becomes easy.

Another Example

We will calculate the recipe for a high-temperature glaze using a chemical formula:

K_2O 0.2 Al_2O_3 0.3
SiO_2 3
MgO   0.8

Determine the materials:

Potassium feldspar $K_2O.Al_2O_3.6SiO_2$
Kaolin $Al_2O_3.2SiO_2$
Talc $3MgO.4SiO_2$
Silica SiO_2

Since one mole of talc has 3MgO, we can calculate the quantity corresponding to the 0.8 MgO of the formula by applying a simple rule of three:

1 ——— 3
x ——— 0.8 $x = 0.8 \times 1 \div 3$

= 0.27 moles of talc

In addition, this material has $4SiO_2$. Thus, the previously obtained result is multiplied by four: $4 \times 0.27 = 1.08$ moles of SiO_2.

The same calculation is repeated for the other materials and step by step, a table like the one below is drawn up to show the contribution of the various materials.

For example, feldspar provides:
0.2 moles of K_2O
0.2 moles of Al_2O_3
1.2 moles of SiO_2 $(6 \times 0.2 = 1.2)$

Kaolin provides:
0.1 moles of Al_2O_3
0.2 moles of SiO_2 $(2 \times 0.1 = 0.2)$

To calculate the recipe, multiply the results by the respective molecular weights:

Talc 0.27×370 $= 99.90$
Feldspar 0.2×556 $= 111.2$
Kaolin 0.1×258 $= 25.8$
Silica 0.52×60 $= 31.2$
                                      268.10

To reduce the recipe to decimals, multiply the results by 100 and divide by the sum:

Talc $99.9 \times 100 \div 268.10 = 37.262$
Feldspar $111.2 \times 100 \div 268.10 = 41.477$
Kaolin $25.8 \times 100 \div 268.10 = 9.623$
Silica $31.2 \times 100 \div 268.10 = 11.637$

Round off the decimals larger than 5 and the recipe will look like this:

Talc ——————— 37
Feldspar ———— 41
Kaolin ————— 10
Silica ——————— 12

materials \ oxides	MgO 0.8	K_2O 0.2	Al_2O_3 0.3	SiO_2 3
Talc 0.27	$0.8 - 0.8 = 0$			$3 - 1.08 = 1.92$
Feldspar 0.2		$0.2 - 0.2 = 0$	$0.3 - 0.2 = 0.1$	$1.92 - 1.2 = 0.72$
Kaolin 0.1			$0.1 - 0.1 = 0$	$0.72 - 0.2 = 0.52$
Silicon 0.52				$0.52 - 0.52 = 0$

TYPES OF GLAZES

There are so many ways of classifying ceramic glazes that every ceramist probably has a different one, although there will be points in common. Glazes can be classified according to their preparation, chemical components, firing temperature, kiln atmosphere, the clay material used, and according to shine, transparency, or texture.

Raw, fritted, or mixed. Raw glazes are prepared with mixed and ground ceramic materials that, after adding water, are applied to both raw and bisque-fired pieces. Their maturing temperatures vary greatly.

Fritted glazes contain materials that are soluble in water and cannot be applied raw, such as sodium, potassium, and borax. These materials are mixed with others and should be fritted in a kiln specially designed for fritting. (Fritting is explained on page 62.) Some glazes are prepared with a mixture of raw and fritted materials and are thus considered "mixed."

Lead-based, alkaline, feldspathic, and the like. For low-temperature firing, glazes are divided into lead-based and alkaline, depending on whether their fluxing agent is lead or alkaline materials, such as sodium or potassium. At high temperatures, on the other hand, if the main

Teapot, 1997. Thrown stoneware, 24 × 14 × 13 cm (9 1/2 x 5 1/2 x 5 1/8 in.). Feldspathic glaze with 3% cobalt oxide. Firing temperature: 1280°C (2336°F).

fluxing agent is feldspar, it is called a feldspathic glaze.

Low, medium, high, or very high firing temperature. Glazes fall into these four temperature groups depending on which temperature they mature at, which is determined by their composition. These criteria are somewhat subjective, but they can be roughly classed as follows. Low-temperature glazes are those that mature between 920 and 1050°C (1688–1922°F). Medium-tem-

Small vase, 1975. Thrown stoneware, 12 × 12 cm (4 3/4 × 4 3/4 in.). Oxidation atmosphere. Firing temperature: 1280°C (2336°F).

Cylinder, 1998. 7.5 x 10.5 cm (3 x 4 1/4 in.). Firing temperature: 1280°C (2336°F).

perature glazes have maturation temperatures from 1050 to 1150°C (1922–2102°F). High-temperature glazes range from 1150 to 1280°C (2102–2336°F) and very-high-temperature glazes range from 1280 to 1400°C (2336–2552°F).

Oxidizers and reducers. Oxidizers are for oxidation kiln atmospheres, especially for electric and gas kilns. Reducers are for reduction kiln atmospheres (those with no oxygen), and are meant for gas, wood, or petroleum kilns. The most practical are gas kilns, whose burners can regulate air and fuel intake. It is not practical to use electric

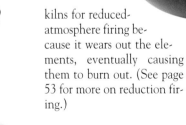

kilns for reduced-atmosphere firing because it wears out the elements, eventually causing them to burn out. (See page 53 for more on reduction firing.)

Glazes for red earthenware, white industrial earthenware, stoneware, and por-

celain clay bodies. Specially adapted for the type of clay they are to be used on, these glazes thus cover an entire range of materials and the temperatures at which they will be fired.

Transparent and opaque. Transparent glazes allow the color of the bisque-fired clay on which they are applied to come through. Opaque glazes, which have opacifying materials mixed into them, do not allow any clay color to show through. There are also two related categories: translucid glazes, which are neither transparent nor opaque since they allow light to pass through but are not

Bowl, 1982. Thrown red earthenware and white industrial earthenware, 8 × 12 cm (3 1/8 × 4 3/4 in.).Transparent glaze. Firing temperature: 960°C (1730°F).

Goblet, 1985. Slab-built stoneware with fine grog, 10 x 7 cm (4 x 2 3/4 in.). Matte glaze. Firing temperature: 1280°C (2336°F).

completely transparent; and opalescent glazes, which have a pearly look.

Gloss, matte, semi-matte, and satin finishes. Glazes with gloss finish look shiny when light reflects off surfaces to which they have been applied. Matte glazes have no sheen. Both gloss and matte glazes can be either transparent or opaque. Semi-matte and satin glazes have a dim sheen and thus lie somewhere between; they are generally opaque.

Smooth and rough. Glazes can have different textures once applied to a surface, depending on their composition and the firing temperature. Such textures can intentionally be brought out by adding materials such as alumina that elevate the fluxing point of a glaze. These are generally matte glazes.

GLAZING EQUIPMENT

Mortar and pestle. Made of glass or porcelain, the mortar is a bowl-like vessel; the pestle shaped something like a small baseball bat. They are used for grinding and mixing glazes.

Sieve. The sieve is nylon or metal mesh. There are many different grades of mesh; the number indicates the number of fibers per square inch: meshes of 40–60 are used for thick materials, 80–100 for fine, and 150 for extremely fine.

Graduated test tubes. Made of glass or plastic, graduated test tubes feature markings to indicate volume measurements. They are very useful for calculating the precise amount of water required to add to clay mixtures or glazes.

Precision scale. This is used for weighing very precise or small amounts, ranging from hundredths of a gram to 50 grams. A spatula or teaspoon is also useful in handling such small amounts.

Spray booth. This booth consists of metal or wooden walls and contains a ventilator or extractor linked to a chimney. It is used for applying glazes with a spraygun. A compressor is also needed.

Slip trailer or engobing bulb. This small rubber syringe is used for applying glazes or engobes.

Scale. This instrument is used for weighing out materials.

PREPARING GLAZES

The process of preparing has three phases: weighing, grinding, and hydrating the materials. Before you begin, you need a glaze recipe and the proper equipment: a set of scales, a glass or porcelain mortar and pestle, a graduated test tube, and a 100-mesh or denser sieve. Following is a sample explanation of the basic process of preparing a small amount of glaze, which will be enough for two examples.

1. Place the ingredients and equipment on a work surface. All the tools must be completely clean. Weigh out the seven ingredients that will form the glaze on the precision scales.

2. After the materials are weighed, grind them with the mortar and pestle. (Always move the pestle in the same circular direction.) Add the coloring oxides and continue grinding until all the components are very well blended.

3. Measure out the right amount of water in a graduated test tube. (As a general rule, 400–500 cc of water is added per kilo of dry ingredients.) Add the coloring oxide and continue blending until the mixture acquires a uniform color.

4. After the materials have been ground together, pass the mixture through a 100-mesh sieve to ensure that it has blended properly. If the glaze will be applied with a spraygun, use a 200-mesh sieve.

5. In this case I am using a brush. Once the mixture is finished passing through the sieve it is ready to be applied on a bisque-fired piece of stoneware.

6. It is helpful to mark a reference on the back of the sample (here I am using iron oxide dissolved in water). With a brush, apply the glaze to the face of the surface of the sample, which must be clean and dry. The glaze layer should be about 2 mm (1/16 in.) thick.

7. These various samples illustrate shapes that are practical for determining whether a glaze will remain in place during the firing process.

GLAZES AND COMMERCIAL CERAMIC PIGMENTS

A wide variety of ceramic pigments is available as the base color for glazes or to be mixed with them. These colors come in powdered form and are frequently used over or under a glaze. They are prepared by mixing with water, and are applied with a brush or a spraygun directly onto bisque-fired clay (ivory white after firing) or onto unfritted glaze.

To reduce the melting point, they may be mixed in a proportion of 10 percent with a glaze or transparent coating. If these pigments are used underneath a glaze, the glaze must be transparent. If used on top, the opaque glaze should completely cover the bisque-fired piece and the color should be applied on top. This method of decoration must be very precise, because there is no way of correcting mistakes once it has been applied. The glaze absorbs the color rapidly, acting as a drying agent.

Ceramic pigments are manufactured in powdered form in an extensive range of colors. Colors can be combined.

Firing temperature depends on the glaze, but it is generally about 940–980°C (1724–1796°F). These colors can be applied to a piece that has been glazed and fired, but in that case the piece will need three firings: a bisque-firing, a glaze firing, and a final firing for the colored decoration.

Commercial Glazes

Industrially manufactured glazes are easy to find in specialty ceramics stores. They come in powdered form in a wide range of colors and assure consistent results if used within their intended temperature ranges. These glazes are made up of low-temperature fluxes, silica and pigments, and they contain very little alumina, if any. They can be combined to produce an extraordinary range of colors and very interesting effects. In addition to water, other fluids can be mixed with the glazes, such as special oils for serigraphy.

Commercial glazes are relatively easy to prepare: just mix them with water (in a proportion of 40–50 percent of their dry weight) until a fluid paste forms. The powder does not have to be ground or passed through a sieve unless it will be applied with a spraygun.

These samples show commercial glazes prepared by mixing the pigment with water and applying it directly to small tiles of red earthenware and white earthenware clay. Firing temperature: 960°C (1760°F).

Medium- and high-temperature glazes are also available. If you are glazing pieces for home use, be sure to consult with the supplier or manufacturer because certain glazes may not comply with safety regulations for everyday items, especially those used for storing or serving food. Also, some glazes are vulnerable to attack by acids in food and drink, and also by alkaline substances in detergents.

These glazes are very practical when making a series of works that require identical colors, especially when you have to replace a missing piece that forms part of a set (tea or coffee sets, or crockery, for instance). Furthermore, they are excellent for use when working with beginners, since it is possible to "see" the color being applied, which is not the case with a prepared glaze.

KILNS AND ACCESSORIES

The kiln is an essential piece of equipment for any ceramicist. Because of the substantial cost, before buying or building a kiln it is important to know what your own particular firing needs will be and to understand the advantages and disadvantages of each type of kiln. There are two basic types: the electric kiln and the gas kiln. The following section discusses which type is most appropriate in terms of the pieces that explained in this book: the number of pieces, their size, their firing temperature, the space available in the studio or workshop, legal requirements, and other relevant considerations.

Electric Kilns

Electric kilns come in square, rectangular, or cylindrical form. Inside the metal-plated exterior are refractory bricks, and between these two materials is a layer of ceramic insulation that prevents heat loss, thereby reducing the amount of power needed for the kiln to reach the required temperature. The electric kiln normally found in a studio is mounted on a base frame with wheels, which makes it easy to move around. In the studio it is a good idea to install it in a fixed spot near a power point. Before purchasing your kiln, be sure you have enough power to run it.

Nowadays many electric kilns run off the domestic power supply, but if your kiln exceeds a certain size it will almost certainly need an extra power source, which can greatly increase the cost.

Electric current passes through the kiln by means of heating elements located in the door, the side walls, and the base, either in grooves or channels cut into the bricks,

1. The top-loading electric kiln is practical and economic to run It has elements inside the two inner walls and can reach temperatures of 1260°C (2300°F). With this type of kiln it is easy to make sure the pots are not touching one another on the sides, but it is not possible to gauge their height from above. To prevent them from sticking to the shelves during glaze firing, a stick of wood is placed across two props to check the height of the pieces before setting the bats, or shelves, in place.

2. This front-loading kiln has heating elements in the side and back walls, the base, and the door. It is equipped with a platinum-rhodium-element (pyrometer) and an electronically operated automatic programming system. It can reach temperatures of up to 1340°C (2444°F). This is one of the safest, easiest to use, and most versatile of all kilns.

or encased in porcelain tubing or other refractory material. The elements spread heat around the interior by means of radiation, and through the ceramics by means of conduction and radiation. The elements are manufactured from alloys of nickel and chrome, and are very long-lasting provided a temperature of 1100°C (2012°F) is not exceeded. Kanthal elements are used to obtain higher temperatures; they are more effective, but soften at high temperatures and are extremely fragile when cold. Because of the extremely high temperatures in even low-temperature kilns, the door features a safety-lock switch so that the machine automatically disconnects if the door opens.

Keep in mind that elements become fragile after many uses, so try not to touch or jar them with the ceramic pieces when loading and unloading the kiln. (A broken element is fairly easy to replace, however.) The elements must also be handled carefully when removing any bits of clay that may have become imbedded in them, such as may happen if a pot explodes in the kiln. Because the kiln is costly and is such an indispensable part of ceramic making, it is important to keep it in good working order. To keep the elements clean, go over them gently with a brush or a small vacuum cleaner, always starting at the uppermost elements. Then remove the dust that has built up on the base plate.

Electric kilns are generally front-loading. Other, less common, models are built in superimposed sections, each section an independent unit with its own elements that can be connected to the others. This type of kiln is very useful because it can be made smaller or larger depending on the number of pots you want to fire.

Electric kilns produce a very clean atmosphere, but generally they should not be used for firings that require a reduction atmosphere. Although they *can* be used for this purpose it is not usually recommended, since the reducing temperature corrodes the metal of the elements, thus shortening their life. (See page 53 for more on reduction firing.)

One of the great advantages of the electric kiln is that since it is automatic it allows you some freedom to concentrate on other things while it is in operation. (You still have to check on the gradual temperature increase; be especially attentive as the final temperature is reached.) Although these machines have very precise pyrometers, in the interests of safety it is well worth setting pyrometric cones in place to ensure the firing process is carried out correctly.

Gas Kilns

Of the fuel-burning types of kiln, gas kilns are the kind most used. They work on either propane or butane. The gas is burned by means of the atmospheric, or aspiration, burner. If you are using bottled gas, as a safety precaution store extra units of gas away from the kiln, somewhere outdoors and protected by a sturdy wall. Just remember that keeping the gas outside can affect the pressure, which means that two sets of bottles are needed.

Like electric kilns, gas kilns are built with a metal outer casing surrounding refractory bricks. Some kilns are lined with insulating fiber, which makes fuel consumption more economical and speeds up the firing and coolingdown processes. Both of these processes are carefully controlled to avoid breakages.

Gas kilns are relatively easy to construct, if the necessary parts are available and if you know how to set up the burners and the downdraft system, which may be direct or cross-draft.

It is important that the flames do not touch the ceramics, so careful consideration must be given to the arrangement of the burners. When loading this type of kiln, leave a space of at least 5 cm (2 in.) between the individual pieces and the walls of the firing chamber.

3. The updraft gas kiln has burners in the three sides, and is fueled by butane or propane gas. The atmosphere may be oxidation, reduction, or neutral, with temperatures rising to 1300°C (2342°F). Firing is from a direct flame.

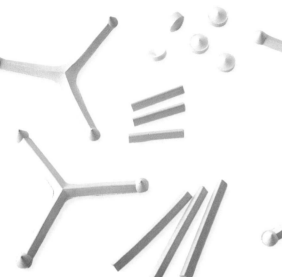

Tile racks. Made of refractory materials, these hold tiles in a way that allows air to circulate around them during firing. The racks can be stacked on top of one another, which is especially useful when there is little space in the kiln.

Stilts, props, and spurs. These items are used to support glazed ceramics in the kiln. Some are star-shaped with pointed tips, some are triangular pieces about 2–3 cm (3/4–1 1/4 in.) long, and some are tubular pieces about 1 cm (3/8 in.) in height and diameter.

Bats or shelves. Made of compact clay with a high aluminum content, silimanite or silicon carbide, and other materials of a high thermal resistance, these support the pots in the kiln and make up stacking racks.

Plate racks. Made of refractory materials, these racks are able to resist very high temperatures. They are useful when firing large numbers of plates, since their stackable design makes good use of the space in the kiln.

Carborundum pillar props. Made of silicon carbide, a refractory material, they resist very high temperatures and conduct heat well.

Pillars and props. These are used to support bats and stacking shelves in the kiln. You will need various sizes. There are two types. The first is made of refractory clay and clay mixed with grog.

Pillars and props. This type is made of porcelain clay. The props are embedded in the collars (shown on the left) to increase the area of the point of contact and distribute the weight more evenly.

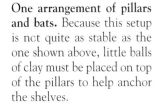

One arrangement of pillars and bats. Because this setup is not quite as stable as the one shown above, little balls of clay must be placed on top of the pillars to help anchor the shelves.

Another arrangement of pillars and bats. This is the most stable of any method of arranging the props and bats; three pillars actually provide greater stability than four.

PACKING THE KILN AND FIRING

Before stacking pots in the kiln, think about how you want to arrange them so you can prepare the bats and support pillars. This is an essential part of the process because the location of the support pillars determines how the pots will be stacked. Three or four support pillars may be used beneath each bat; if you use four, remember to place a small ball of clay on top of each one to increase stability. All the pillars of each level must be the same height, though the heights of different levels can vary.

A glaze firing requires even greater care than does a firing of unglazed pots. Make sure that the bottoms of all the pots are clean and free of any extra specks of glaze; there may be spillage with a glaze that has a low temperature or fusion margin. Stack the pieces on spurs without

The packed kiln, after firing. Note the alumina-based tiles placed under the pieces. At bottom center, a pillar supports a bent-over pyrometric cone, which indicates that the correct firing temperature has been reached.

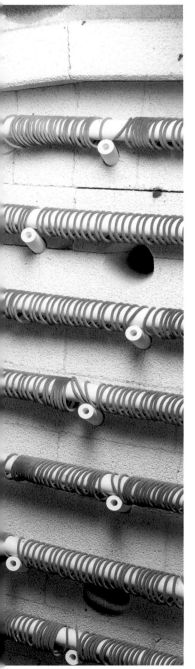

letting them touch the support tile. If necessary, stand the pots on bisque-fired tiles coated with an alumina-based wash or silica and kaolin. This simple and cheap covering prevents the bats from breaking in the case of spillage.

If you are using an electric kiln, it is best to leave about 3 cm (1 1/4 in.) between the kiln and the pieces to be fired. Remember that glaze melts during firing, so items must be far enough apart to avoid sticking together, and so that the more volatile colors of certain glazes do not spoil other pots in the vicinity.

Glazes boil when they reach their melting point, so you must be particularly careful not to turn off the kiln at this moment or your glaze will emerge covered in bubbles. If the fusion temperature is exceeded, the glaze may start to run, causing the piece to stick to the supporting bat beneath it.

Firing

All pieces to be fired should be completely dry, whether they are raw or glazed. Damp pieces should never be fired in the kiln because as the temperature increases, the pressure of the evaporating

water may cause unfired pots to explode, or may cause the coating on glazed pieces to separate, resulting in uneven glazing.

It is important to remember that making a ceramic piece from start to finish is a slow process, from preparing the clay and modeling the work to mixing and applying the glaze to various firing stages. Trying to economize on time or fuel can cost more than it saves—if the proper methods are not followed you will have wasted your time, effort, and materials on a ruined piece. Even though the process of firing glazed ceramics is faster than firing raw pieces, it must still be

carried out slowly. With an electric kiln, remember to allow the escape of water that has been introduced during the application of glaze. With a gas kiln, you can leave the door ajar. At 200°C (392°F), the glaze loses any water and at the same time burns off any adhesives. This slow pace must be maintained, since cristobalite expands at about 300°C (572°F), quartz at 500°C. At approximately 600°C (1112°F), the rate of heating can be faster, and continue thus until the glaze reaches its melting point.

Generally, in a kiln measuring 50 cm (20 in.) square, the firing process of a low-

temperature glaze takes about 8 hours, depending on the number of pieces stacked in the kiln. Firing glazed stoneware pieces in the same kind of kiln requires at least 12 hours at a temperature of 1280°C (2336°F). When the fusion point of the glaze is reached the oven is turned off, producing a rapid reduction in the temperature, which later stabilizes. Special care should be taken when it reaches the critical zones, since when the kiln cools down the process can be inverted. Allow the kiln to cool off completely—do not open it until the pots can be removed by hand without fear of burns.

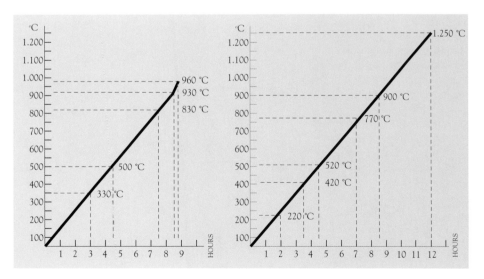

Graphs showing two firings in an electric kiln, one at low temperature and the other at high temperature. Final temperatures: 960 and 1250°C (1730 and 2282°F).

TEMPERATURE AND COLOR CONSIDERATIONS

Regardless of the firing method used, it is important to control the kiln temperature as precisely as possible. This can be done through various systems of measurement: a pyrometer, pyrometric cones, or the color of the flames. Another method, rarely used these days, is to fire small samples of glazed ceramic that are removed one by one to see if the glaze has melted yet. This system requires a kiln with an aperture large enough through which to insert an iron rod to reach the samples.

This temperature controller can be digitally programmed to regulate the duration of a firing, the temperature and its rate of ascent, and the cut-off points.

The Pyrometer

A pyrometer is an instrument used to measure the temperature inside the kiln. It operates through the use of a thermocouple, two metal threads soldered together at one end. For high-temperature firing these threads must be made of a platinum-rhodium alloy; for low-temperature firing a chrome-nickel alloy is sufficient. The metal threads are generally encased in a porcelain shell enclosed in the kiln. The ends of the thermocouple that extend outside the kiln are connected to a meter by a cable so the circuit remains closed. As the thermocouple heats up, a small amount of voltage is used, which is measured on a galvanometer by reading the graduated scale showing degrees of temperature.

There are also pyrometers equipped with a mechanism that shuts down the kiln automatically when the required temperature is reached. Nowadays, electronic pyrometers with digital displays are fairly common.

Pyrometric Cones

Pyrometric cones allow the ceramist to establish very precisely not just the kiln temperature, but also the time-temperature ratio. These measuring devices come in the form of pyramids with a triangular base; they bear a number on each face, ranging from 022 (600°C) to 42 (2000°C). Made of ceramic materials, they are designed so that they fold over at predetermined temperatures.

Pyrometric cones were created in the nineteenth century by the German chemist Hermann Seger. Seger cones are used in Europe, but American ceramicists use Orton pyrometric cones. They have a similar numbering scale, but the corresponding temperatures are different. Seger cones used at low temperatures contain fluxes; those used for high-temperature firing employ more refractory materials. Note that cones work well in an oxidation atmosphere but not in a reduction one. (See page 53 for more on reduction firing.)

Cones should be placed in the kiln where they can be

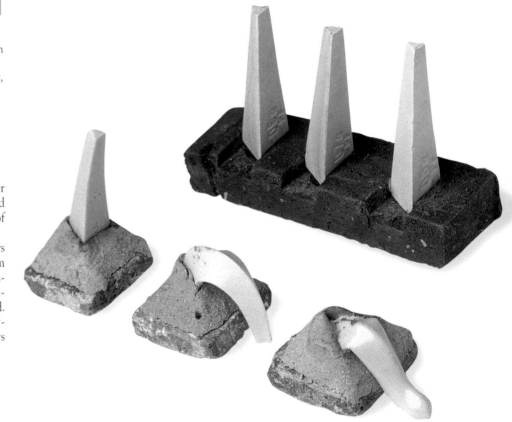

Pyrometric cones are manufactured from a mixture of ceramic materials and are designed to fold over at a certain temperature. These elongated pyramids are intended to be used at a heating up rate of 150°C (302°F) per hour. It is advisable to use three cones with a correlative number scale when firing.

Seger Cones			Orton Cones	
Nº	Temperature °C	Temperature °F	Temperature °C	Temperature °F
022	600	1112	600	1112
021	650	1202	614	1137
020	670	1238	635	1175
019	690	1274	683	1261
018	710	1310	717	1323
017	730	1346	747	1377
016	750	1382	792	1458
015 a	790	1454	804	1479
014 a	815	1499	838	1540
013 a	835	1535	852	1566
012 a	855	1571	884	1623
011 a	880	1616	894	1641
010 a	900	1652	894	1641
09 a	920	1688	923	1693
08 a	940	1724	955	1751
07 a	960	1760	984	1803
06 a	980	1796	999	1830
05 a	1000	1832	1046	1915
04 a	1020	1868	1060	1940
03 a	1040	1904	1101	2014
02 a	1060	1940	1120	2048
01 a	1080	1976	1137	2079
1 a	1100	2012	1154	2109
2 a	1120	2048	1162	2124
3 a	1140	2084	1168	2134
4 a	1160	2120	1186	2167
5 a	1180	2156	1196	2185
6 a	1200	2192	1222	2232
7	1230	2246	1240	2264
8	1250	2282	1263	2305
9	1280	2336	1280	2336
10	1300	2372	1305	2381
11	1320	2408	1315	2399
12	1350	2462	1326	2419
13	1380	2516	1346	2455
14	1410	2570	1366	2491
15	1435	2615	1431	2608

Table relating to the Seger and Orton systems of pyrometric cones showing the reference number and corresponding temperature in degrees Centigrade and Fahrenheit.

seen through the peephole in the kiln. (It is very important to protect your eyes from the heat, and you should have a sheet of glass over the hole to filter out the infrared rays.) Place the cones on a lump of clay at an 8° angle from the bat, so they bend over as soon as the required temperature has been reached. When the upper face of the bent cone touches the bat, it is time to switch off the kiln. Once a cone has been used, even if it has not doubled over, it cannot be used again.

Pyrometric cones are generally prepared to heat up at a rate of 150°C (302°F) per hour, but if this rhythm is accelerated the cone will take longer to double over. Conversely, if the firing has been slow, the cone will double over before the required temperature is reached. Although the pyrometer might indicate that the temperature is not yet high enough, if the cone bends over it is a good idea to switch off the kiln. Glazes do not fuse at a precise temperature and a glaze subjected to a prolongated firing will fuse prematurely.

The condition of a cone is an indication of the state of firing. A swollen cone, for instance, may point to a firing being carried out too quickly or one that is insufficiently oxidized, while a roughened surface or split edge indicates that sulphurous vapors from the fuel have been released during the firing. These indications may also be due to an excess of water vapor at the start of the firing.

Conversion Formula

On the Centigrade scale, the melting point of ice corresponds to 0° and the boiling point of water to 100°. On the Fahrenheit scale, these temperatures are 32° and 212° respectively.

Converting Centigrade into Fahrenheit
Example: $100°C \times 9/5 = 180$
$180 + 32 = 212°F$
Converting Fahrenheit into Centigrade
Example: $212°F - 32 = 180$
$180 \times 5/9 = 100°C$

The relationship between degrees Centigrade and degrees Fahrenheit can be expressed by this formula:
$°C/100 = °F - 32/180$

For example, 800°C = 1472°F, as follows:
$800/100 = °F - 32/180$
$800 \times 180 = 100°F - 3200$
$144,000 + 3200 = 100°F$
$147,200 = 100°F$
$°F = 147,200 \div 100 = 1472$

When you are learning about firing, as a precautionary measure you can place various cones on different levels within the kiln. This will enable you to judge the small or significant differences in temperature that may exist inside the kiln. The cones can also used in threes, on a graduated number scale. If you want a firing of 960°C (1730°F), for instance, you can place an 08a (940°C/1724°F) cone on one side, an 07a (960°C/1730°F) in the middle, and an 06a (980°C/1796°F) on the other side. The first should double over completely and even begin to melt, the second should form a perfect arch, and the third should stay upright. In this way, you gauge with accuracy whether the firing temperature is the right one.

Color Changes During Firing

When firing pieces of the same or similar kind, it is useful to be able to interpret changes in the color of the flame as an indication of the temperature of the firing process, but this can only be learned through observation and experience. Temperatures must be very precise when firing glazed pieces, so it is advisable to use one of the methods previously described.

These colors are only visible in an oxidation atmosphere. Up to 500°C (1022°F), there will be no color inside the kiln. Between 550 and 600°C (1022–1112°F), the kiln will look dull red, which deepens between 600 and 700°C (1112–1292°F), and finally becomes deep red around 790°C (1454°F). From this point on the deep red begins to turn cherry red, a color that becomes fully developed at 880°C (1616°F). At 980°C (1796°F), it is a paler cherry, tending toward orange, which turns brilliant between 1000 and 1080°C (1832–1976°F). At around 1180°C (2156°F) it is pale orange and becomes paler still at 1250°C (2282°F). At 1280°C (2336°F) the color changes from pale yellow to yellowish white. Between 1300 and 1350°C (2342–2462°F) it is yellowish white, and it becomes a dazzling white at 1380°C (2516°F). At around 1480–1500°C (2696–2732°F) the color is a brilliant, dazzling white with a bluish haze.

GLAZING WITH THE DIPPING METHOD

The Basics of Glaze Application

There are four ways of applying glaze: dipping, pouring, painting, and spraying. All pieces can be glazed using any one of these methods, but you should consider the shape and size of each piece and choose the method that is most appropriate. Novice ceramists should begin with the painting method. In addition to choosing the correct method, it is useful to know about the thickness of application. Glazes applied too thickly can crack or run, and a layer of varying consistency will not vitrify.

Transparent glazes require a very fine layer, between 0.7 and 1 mm (1/48–1/32 in.). If the piece has a motif or decoration, this glaze must allow it to remain visible. A thicker layer will produce a milky glaze that will lose its transparency. Opaque glazes must be thicker, about 1.5 mm (1/24 in.), and the crystalline type must be applied in denser layers of 2 to 4 mm (1/16–5/32 in.).

Dipping

Dipping is perhaps the best system for glazing a series of similar pieces because the glaze is uniform over the entire surface. It is fast, simple, and does not waste glaze. But the glaze must be prepared to the right density and applied in the right thickness. Study the way the glaze takes hold of each piece and the time the pot needs to be submerged in the glaze solution. With a bit of experience, this understanding comes quickly.

Choose a container that is large enough to accommodate the piece to be glazed. Remember that the piece will displace the glaze when it is dipped into the container and the glaze will rise up the container sides, so be sure to choose a container large enough to allow for this increase in volume.

The piece must be completely clean before it is glazed so that the solution adheres properly. First, coat the inside: pour the glaze directly into the piece so that it fills the piece at least halfway. (Rather than lift the large glaze container, fill a smaller container with glaze and pour from that one.) Twist and turn the piece until the glaze covers the entire inner surface, then pour the excess glaze back into the container. Rotate the piece while pouring the glaze back into the container to coat up to the rim. Grasp the piece by the neck and dip in the glaze; hold it there for a few seconds, then slowly raise it out of the glaze with an up-and-down movement. Let it stand on the work surface while you repeat the operation to glaze other pieces. (Be sure to stir the solution after each dipping to prevent the glaze from settling out of the water and thus resulting in diluted solution at the top of the container.)

When the glaze appears completely matte with no shiny, damp patches, pick up the piece with clean hands, holding it by the glazed part. Dip the unglazed part into the solution until it meets the part that is already coated. Follow the same procedure as before, then return it to the work surface until the glaze has dried. When the glaze is dry to the touch, clean the base with a stiff brush or a scraper to remove any glaze residue. If touchups are needed on the edges, apply some glaze with a paintbrush.

Be aware of how long the piece is submerged in the solution. If left too long the glaze layer may be too thick, or it may wash off because it has not sufficiently adhered to the piece.

1. Prepare the glaze in the proper container. If necessary, pass the glaze through a sieve to remove the lumps. To glaze the inside of a piece with a narrow opening, pour the glaze from a smaller container into a funnel set in the neck of the piece.

2. Twist the piece to coat the inside, taking care not to spill the glaze. Pour the remaining glaze back into the container. Pouring it over the edge of a spatula prevents it from forming sediment on the bottom.

3. Grasp the neck of the piece and dip it in the glaze. Do not allow the glaze to reach your fingers. Repeat the operation about three times, until the glaze acquires the necessary thickness. Set the piece on the work surface until the glaze is dry to the touch.

4. Stir the glaze again and, holding the piece by its base, submerge it twice, as far as the line of the part already glazed.

5. Set the piece aside again until it is dry to the touch. Note that the dampness makes the glaze look shiny.

6. Once the glaze is dry to the touch, clean the base with a small, stiff-bristled brush. If you put the jar on a stilt and place that on a small bisque-fired tile, you will not have to touch the piece directly when placing it in the kiln. Remember that dry, unfired glaze peels away easily, so never handle it while in this state.

7. The finished piece shows the smooth glaze application possible with the dipping method.

Greenish Blue, 1998. Thrown earthenware clay, 24.5 × 11 cm (9 3/4 × 4 3/8 in.). Commercial glaze with blue and green pigments. Firing temperature: 980°C (1796°F).

GLAZING WITH THE POURING METHOD

The pouring method of glazing is popular with many ceramists because it is economical and quick. It requires a wide, flat container and two iron rods or wooden strips. To further ease glaze application, this container can be placed on a banding wheel, so that it—and thus the piece—can be turned while the glaze solution is poured over.

The piece must be completely clean before it is glazed so that the solution adheres properly. First, coat the inside of the piece, as in the dipping method: partially filled the piece with glaze and turn it so the glaze evenly coats the inner surface, then pour out the excess glaze. If the piece is a vase or similar form, coat the rim next, by immersing it directly in the glaze just an inch or so. Next, stand the piece upright on the rods or strips. Begin pouring on the glaze, starting with the coated part (the rim), turning the piece (or preferably the banding wheel) with your free hand. Do not let the lip of the glaze container come into contact with the surface of the piece. While you are pouring, make sure the glaze flows evenly over the surface with good coverage and no drips (unless, of course, you specifically want a drip effect). When the pot is dry to the touch, clean the base with a stiff brush or a scraper to remove any glaze residue.

The first coating of glaze will not be thick enough to produce a good finish on larger pieces, so a second layer will be needed on top of the first. Applying the glaze in two layers will produce a much nicer finish than trying to accomplish the task in one, thicker layer. The second layer should be applied as soon as the first layer is dry to the touch; do not wait any longer or the glaze will bubble and may even craze or crack. If desired, the second layer can be a different glaze than the first one for an interesting effect.

Bisque-fired pieces should be kept in a dust-free environment or should be covered. Before glazing, dust them off with a brush; try not to handle them too much because the sweat from your hands may prevent the glaze from adhering. Before applying the glaze, you can dampen the pieces with a moist sponge or run them very briefly under a faucet to prevent thick layers of glaze from forming later on.

1. Prepare the glaze and pour some into the piece, filling it about halfway.

2. Holding the piece with both hands (be sure your hands are clean and dry), rotate it so the glaze covers the entire inner surface. This movement must be fairly rapid so that a thick coat of glaze does not form on the bottom, and must be done without interruption so that the glaze does not drip or run over the outer surface (unless you intentionally want this effect).

3. Place two iron rods (or wood strips) over a wide, shallow container and set the piece upside down over this, resting on the rods. Pour the glaze evenly over the surface to the appropriate thickness. When the piece has been completely covered, let it sit until it is dry to the touch.

4. Turn the piece over and pour glaze over the outside, taking care not to drip glaze into the interior. Once again, let it sit until it is dry to the touch.

5. Holding the piece with one hand, remove the excess glaze from the base with a scraper or a stiff brush. Finish the cleaning with a wet sponge.

6. This is what the glaze looks like after it has been fired.

Pot, 1998.
Thrown stoneware, 21 × 11 cm
(8 1/8 × 4 3/8 in.)
Feldspar glaze with 3% iron oxide and dolomite.
Firing temperature: 1260°C (2300°F).

GLAZING WITH A BRUSH

The brush method is used for pieces that are to be glazed in various colors, and also for decorative touches. This technique is especially appropriate for glazing murals, sculptures, or reliefs, since more than one type of glaze is often required and the method allows for greater precision in defining the different areas. It is also used for pieces with a crystalline glaze, which requires a thicker application than other types. Novice ceramists should begin with the brush technique; although it does require some experience, the skill is fairly easy to acquire with some practice. Experience will teach you how much glaze to apply and how best to take advantage of the glazing possibilities each piece offers.

The glaze is generally applied with a flat brush, about 3 cm (1 1/4 in.) wide, especially if you are glazing the piece with a single color. The brush should be well coated in glaze. Keep in mind that you're really not *painting* with the brush; the object is to achieve good, even coverage, allowing the bisque-fired clay to absorb the glaze and trying not to let it to drip. Use a finer brush to coat any nooks and crannies that a larger brush cannot reach. Be sure to have a different brush for each color of glaze you are using.

Before glazing, gently wash the piece to remove all traces of dust. The water will also keep the bisque-fired ware from absorbing the glaze too quickly and will prevent a wide brush from leaving too thick an application of glaze. To avoid the bisque-fired clay absorbing the glaze too quickly (thus resulting in uneven coverage), it is a good idea to apply a first layer or wash with a fairly watery glaze solution. Be sure this first layer covers the entire surface well, including all the hollows and pores. Wait until this layer is dry to the touch before applying a second layer of glaze. Also, when adding subsequent layers, take care that the brush does not disturb the previous applications of glaze.

The piece may need two or three layers of glaze before it is properly covered. To avoid bubbling or peeling, wait until a layer is dry to the touch before applying a successive layer. For the best coverage, alternate the directions of the layers: if the first one is applied vertically, make the next horizontal. Remember to stir the mixture often during the glazing process so the glaze does not settle on the bottom of the container, leaving a very watery solution on top. Once the glaze has dried to the touch, if parts are uneven, you can smooth over the surface with your fingertip or a thicker-haired brush.

1. Here is everything needed to glaze this cylindrical piece (which was hand-built, with small areas of relief added): banding wheel and tile, flat brushes and paintbrushes, and mortars and pestles containing the glazes. I have chosen brilliant white for the interior and matte white for the exterior, plus light blue, dark blue, garnet, and orange-yellow.

2. Clean all dust off the piece, then wet it. Pour the chosen glaze inside the piece.

3. Rotate the piece with your hands to coat the interior completely. With the same rotating movement, remove any excess glaze.

4. Apply the chosen glaze to the outside of the piece. Here I am using a fairly small brush because the reliefs would render a wider brush useless.

5. Place the piece on a tile set on the banding wheel and continue glazing. Here I am applying prepared iron oxide (Fe_2O_3) in one of the relief areas.

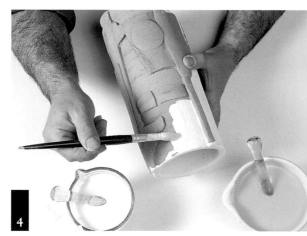

Untitled, 1992.
Slab-built grog stoneware
with reliefs, 27 × 11 cm
(10 5/8 × 4 3/8 in.).
Firing temperature:
1250°C (2282°F).

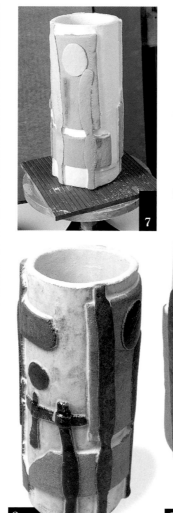

6. Next I apply the light blue glaze with 2 percent cobalt oxide (CoO). When the glazing is finished, store the leftover glaze in sealed bottles and wash the mortars and pestles thoroughly.

7. The glazed cylindrical piece is ready for the kiln.

8 and 9. After firing, the glazed piece looks like this.

GLAZING WITH A SPRAYGUN

Glazing with a spraygun requires more complicated equipment than other methods: a spraygun, a spray booth with a ventilator, a compressor, and a safety mask are all essential. In addition, you'll need a banding wheel on which to place the piece so it can be rotated as you spray the glaze, to achieve smoother, more even coverage.

To keep the spraygun from clogging, the glaze solution must be passed through a 100-mesh sieve or finer. The solution should contain a good suspension agent so it does not leave a sediment in the spraygun reservoir. While spraying, from time to time you can block the air cap with your finger while pressing the lever; the compressed air will pass into the reservoir, bubbling up and stirring the solution.

The nozzle can either release the glaze in jets, or cover large areas of any shape. Always hold the spraygun perpendicular to the piece at a distance of about 30 cm (12 in.). Any farther and the drops of glaze will dry in the air before making contact with the piece; any closer and blotchy stains will result or the glaze will be too wet and thus will not vaporize properly on the surface. If that happens, stop spraying for a few minutes (long enough for the surface to absorb the dampness) and then continue.

When using the spray technique I always apply six layers of glaze to achieve the desired thickness. Since this depends to some degree on the thickness of the glaze, you should experiment to see what works best for you.

Because of the overspray, this glazing method is more wasteful than others; there is a glaze loss of 50–70 percent. However, the excess can be recouped and reused. Since the mix of so many oxidants will produce dark colors, it's best to save it for glazing the interiors of pieces, especially those with very narrow necks where the inside will not be very visible. Lining the booth with a piece of semi-rigid plastic sheeting helps in recovering glaze.

Note that raw lead glazes should never be used with the spraygun glazing technique.

1. As with other glazing methods, begin by preparing the glaze, sieving it, and pouring some into the piece.

2. Holding the piece in both hands, rotate it so the glaze covers the entire inner surface, taking care not to splash any out.

3. Continue to rotate the piece, making sure the glaze covers the rim. Pour the leftover glaze back into the glaze container.

4. Place the piece upside down on the banding wheel. (Here I have placed two triangular "stilts" on the wheel so it has the least possible contact with the piece. To prevent the inner part of the base from being glazed, I have placed a circle of paper over the area and weighted it down a tile.) After donning safety gear, fill the gun's reservoir, turn on the ventilator and the compressor, and aim the gun. Begin turning the banding wheel with your other hand just before you squeeze the trigger so the jet of glaze doesn't concentrate on one spot on the surface.

5. Let the piece sit until the glaze is dry to the touch, then turn it over and continuing glazing, covering the entire surface. Apply as many layers as needed, allowing each to dry to the touch before applying the next. Once the piece is dry after the final glazing, clean the base as in the other methods.

6. After coming out of the kiln, the piece looks like this.

3

4

5

Cup, 1998.
Thrown stoneware
with fine grog,
32 × 30 cm
(12 5/8 × 11 7/8 in.).
Feldspathic glaze with
4% cobalt oxide.
Firing temperature:
1260°C (2300°F).

6

TESTING FOR AND CORRECTING GLAZING DEFECTS

Before beginning to glaze finished pieces, it is important to study the behavior of glazes. Various defects can occur: pinholing or flecking, blistering or bubbling, spillage, glazes with insufficient thickness or ones that have been fired too long, stains, peeling, spitting, and other mishaps. Though it may at first seem like extra work, by performing these tests you will avoid much trouble later on. The tests will reveal any potential problems, and will

also give you an idea of the final results. If you skip this step you risk finding undesired surprises when you open the kiln to retrieve your piece.

So, in addition to calculating glaze formulas and mixing components, you must test-fire them. Prepare a small slab of the clay with which you are going to work; a 6 x 4 cm (2 3/8 × 1 5/8 in.) slab that is 3 to 5 mm (1/8–3/16 in.) thick should be sufficient, although it need not be a specific shape. Once the body has been bisque-fired, cover it with the glaze you want to test. Let it dry, then place it in the kiln and fire it to maturing temperature.

With experience, a rapid analysis of these test pieces will indicate if they can be rectified or not. Set aside those that cannot be retouched for a more in-depth study later on, and concentrate on those that can be resolved. Observation and study will teach you the best course of action.

Spillage is also a problem in ceramics. Pieces can be ruined if they become stuck to the bats, and even the kiln can become unusable if substances drip onto the elements. A simple way to prevent this is to place tiles covered in alumina or a layer of clay or kaolin below the glazed pieces in the kiln in case they drip. Another precaution is to leave the area around the base unglazed.

Pinholes (Flecking)

As water evaporates during the first stage of firing, it may come through the coat of glaze and leave tiny pores akin to pinholes. This defect occurs when the piece is fired too quickly, or when gases are produced within the clay body. It can also happen if the glaze has not dried enough before firing.

If the piece has been fired too little, the pinholes can be rectified by firing the ware again, at the glaze's maturing temperature, or by increasing the temperature a little. Another possible solution is to increase the amount of flux added to the glaze.

Blisters

Blisters can be caused by excess water, either in the clay or in the glaze. Glazing with a spraygun can also cause blistering, especially

Detail of cracked glaze.

Detail of pinholes that resulted when the piece was fired too soon, before the glaze had sufficiently dried.

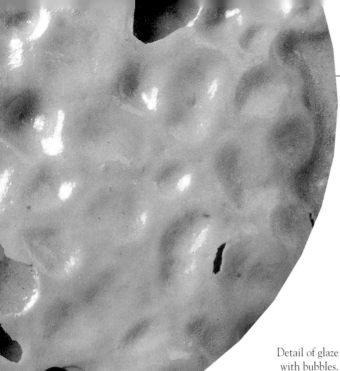

Detail of glaze with bubbles.

ture is exceeded; in other words, they are overfired. When testing glazes, it is worthwhile to study this phenomenon on samples placed vertically, especially on glazes with which you are unfamiliar. The best solution for glazes with a tendency to crawl is to alter the formula by adding alumina, which increases the fusion point.

Some problems can be avoided by firing pieces with glazes that have a similar fusion margin; otherwise some may melt while others have yet to reach their melting point, resulting in crawling as well as blisters.

It is also important to remember that a very slow firing makes the glaze mature more quickly, while a fast firing slows down the fusion.

It is practical to use pyrometric cones in such cases, since they indicate more exactly when the optimum temperature has been reached.

Another significant cause is the application of too thick a layer of glaze, which crawls even when the firing temperature is correct. If you suspect this is the cause, try applying thinner layers.

when applied over a coat of dry glaze. If this happens, try applying the successive layer while the previous one is still damp.

Glazes boil before they reach their fusion point, so if the kiln is turned off during the process before that point is reached, a multitude of bubbles will appear like craters over the surface of the piece once it is removed from the kiln. Sometimes certain oxides, such as magnesite bioxide, can cause bubbling in the glaze, therefore it is necessary to calcinate it before mixing it with other ingredients.

Glazes that are applied too thickly may bubble, especially on this inside of the pieces. This can be avoided by applying a thinner layer and firing more slowly.

Crazing or Cracks

Crazing or cracks can form on the surface of the glaze if its rate of expansion is greater than that of the clay. Other possible causes of this defect are too thick a layer of glaze or letting the kiln cool down too fast.

The best way to rectify this problem is to adjust the clay and/or the glaze so they expand at the same rate. The clay can be modified to shrink more so that the glaze contracts less.

"Crackle" glaze is a specific desired effect, used for decorative purposes.

Crawling

Generally, glazes "crawl" when their fusion tempera-

Placing the piece on a tile covered with alumina will prevent it from sticking to the kiln. Note the way the glaze is running, as well as the area on the left that barely contains any glaze.

Glaze applied using the dipping technique.

Incorrect Thickness of the Glaze Layer

Sometimes you may find you have applied a layer of glaze that is too thin, especially when glazing with a brush that is not appropriate for the circumstances. Or, during the pouring or dipping process, the glaze solution may have settled on the bottom of the glaze container, leaving the upper portion too watery. So remember to stir the glaze often.

Problems can also occur when glazing pieces that have not been bisque-fired properly. Since such pieces are more porous, they tend to absorb more glaze in certain areas than in others, resulting in an uneven finish. The best way to avoid this is to fire the bisque clay at a higher temperature than the glaze, except with pieces that require high-temperature firing.

Pieces with too little glaze can often be rectified if they are glazed and fired again.

brush, which will make for uneven application and will remove new glaze as you work).

The heat given off by the piece will evaporate the water in the glaze, thus helping the glaze adhere. This application will easily come away, so to avoid touching it, before glazing place the piece on a bat that can be used to transport it to the kiln.

If the glaze layer appears too thick, there is little that can be done to remedy it. Study the piece to see if the piece is worth trying to save or whether you should start over. When glazing, pay particular attention to the thickness of the glaze in the piece's interior, since the glaze has a tendency to pool at the bottom.

However, touching up glazed pieces is very labor-intensive because the glaze will not stick since the piece is no longer porous. The only solution is to heat up the piece to 150–200°C (302–360°F) and then spray the glaze on the surface (do not use a

Detail of underfired glaze.

Incorrect Firing Time

If the glaze has not reached its temperature, it will be underfired and it will have a matte, hard aspect and may even have blisters; the color

will not be correct either. Therefore, it is indispensable to know the firing temperature of the glaze you are using as well as kiln type, as the firing will be different according to the size of the kiln, and within a large-size one, there will always be sig-

Although this stain was not planned, it does blend in with the whole, showing that occasionally a defect can result in a positive outcome.

Top and bottom, detail of defects. In both cases the layer of glaze applied was too thick.

nificant temperature differences between the top and bottom shelves, therefore the temperature control must be very precise. In this type of firing, you need to work with glazes with a wider fusion margin, so that they all have enough time to mature without any of them displaying defects.

These glazes can be fired a second time until they reach their maturing temperature, thus producing, in principal, an optimum result. If, on the other hand, the glaze is overfired, it is almost certain to have such bad defects that it will be very difficult to rectify them.

Stains

Stains may occur from contaminants, introduced either during the mixing of the glaze ingredients or within the kiln. These drawbacks can be easily avoided by controlling the mixtures more carefully and by cleaning the mixing vessels and implements and the kiln.

Coloring oxides that become volatile during firing can stain a piece or affect the glaze color of adjacent pieces. When dealing with glazes whose components are susceptible to staining, the best way to avoid the prob-

lem is to keep the pieces separated in the kiln or even fire them at different times.

Separation and Wrinkling

Separation and wrinkling can result when pieces are fired before they have been allowed to dry sufficiently, or if they are dusty or dirty.

Glaze applied too thickly can also cause these defects.

This problem is complicated to retouch. The only solution is to heat up the piece and apply the glaze with a spraygun (see "Incorrect Thickness" above). The best solution is to avoid the problem in the first place by allowing the glaze enough drying time, and/or by cleaning the piece before firing.

Sample showing glaze separation.

Shrinkage

A shrinkage problem occurs when the clay shrinks more than the glaze does, causing the glaze to separate from the bisque-fired piece. This can be avoided by adding a greater proportion of feldspar to the clay body and reducing the amount of quartz. Also, fire the body at a higher temperature and reduce the proportion of calcium carbonate.

LOW- AND MEDIUM-TEMPERATURE GLAZES

Low-Temperature Glazes

Low-temperature glazes can be applied on any type of clay body, although they are generally used on red clay, earthenware. and stoneware. These glazes are divided into two groups: lead glazes and alkaline glazes.

Lead is the main flux in lead glazes. It melts at 410°C (770°F), or between cone 018 (710°C/ 770°F) and cone 2a (1120°C/ 2048°F). The fluxes of these glazes are lead oxide (minimum) Pb_3O_4, and lead carbonate (white lead) $2PbCO_3.Pb(OH)_2$. These materials are highly toxic and must be used with extreme caution; they should not be inhaled, ingested, or even touched with your bare hands.

For this reason, lead is fritted and becomes lead silica. During the frit, the lead and silica melt simultaneously and are then pulverized, producing a nontoxic glaze that is insoluble in water.

Always take great care when working with glazes containing lead.

Glaze Recipes

Cone 08a–07a (940–960°C/1724–1730°F)

Lead oxide	70
Silica	30
Lead oxide	58
Silica	5
Kaolin	7
Tin oxide	10

Alkaline glazes have similar temperature requirements, melting between cones 016 (750°C/ 1382°F) and 02a (1060°C/ 1940°F). Their principal fluxes are alkaline substances such as borax, colemanite (calcium borate), and sodium carbonate. Alkaline ingredients are highly soluble, so they are fritted to obtain insoluble silicates, resulting a group of glazes that appear similar to lead glazes but with colors more in the pastel range.

Bowl, 1997.
Strip-built earthenware, pieces of body modeled with looped tool, placed in plastic receptacle that acts as a mold, 12.5 × 21 cm (5 × 8 1/4 in.). Firing temperature: 1160°C (2120°F).

Glaze Recipes

Cones 05a–03a (1000–1040°C/1802–1904°F)

Silica	55
Lithium carbonate	28
Kaolin	15
Bentonite	2
Colemanite	40
Nepheline syenite	35
Calcium carbonate	15
Silica	10

Medium-Temperature Glazes

These glazes melt in the range of cones 02a and 6a (1060–1200°C/1940–2162°F) and should be used on more compact ceramics, including red clay to cone 2a, as well as on earthenware and stoneware bodies.

Samples of lead glazes, colored with oxides and applied to red clay. Firing temperature: 960 °C (1730°F).

Bottle 1, 1987.
Hollowed-out red clay,
24 x 7 cm (9 1/2 × 2 3/4 in.).
Lead glaze with 3%
cobalt oxide and 5%
natural color.
Firing temperature:
1000°C (1802°F).

Bottle 2, 1987.
Slab-built red clay,
25.5 × 8 cm
(10 × 3 1/8 in.).
Lead glaze with
3% magnesium bioxide
and 5% natural color.
Firing temperature:
1000°C (1802°F).

Cup, 1997.
Slab-built earthenware,
13 × 12.5 cm (5 1/8 × 5 in.).
Firing temperature: 1160°C
(2120°F).

These glaze compositions can use low-temperature fluxes, such as lead and alkaline fluxes, as well as high-temperature fluxes, such as feldspar. These fluxes must be modified, adding more refractory materials in the former and reducing the fusion point in the latter, so that they melt within the temperature margins indicated. Among the ingredients that can be added to these glazes are borax, calcium carbonate, magnesium, colemanite, cryolite, dolomite, spodumene, fluorite, lepidolite zinc oxides, zirconium, titanium, petalite, talc, and wolastonite.

Tray, 1997.
Slab- and strip-built earthenware,
23 x 25 x 11 cm (9 x 9 7/8 x 4 3/8 in.).
Firing temperature: 1160°C (2120°F).

Glaze Recipes

Cone 1a (1100°C/2012°F)
Lead oxide (minimum)	60
Silica	25
Kaolin	15

Cone 4a (1160°C/2120°F)
Nepheline syenite	45
Silica	27
Kaolin	10
Calcium carbonate	8
Magnesium carbonate	5
Zinc oxide	5

Cone 6a (1200°C/2162°F)
Potasium feldspar	46
Kaolin	19
Silica	17
Talc	10
Calcium carbonate	4
Zinc oxide	4

Nepheline syenite	64
Calcium carbonate	15
Kaolin	13
Talc	4
Zinc oxide	4

HIGH AND VERY-HIGH-TEMPERATURE GLAZES

These glazes are applied to types of clay that vitrify, such as stoneware, and are fired at temperatures that range from cones 6a to 9 (1200–1280°C/2162–2336°F). These glazes can be made with very few ingredients. Since their principal flux is feldspar, they are also known as fledspathic glazes, although other materials used as fluxes are calcium carbonate, zinc oxide, dolomite, and talc. Pieces using these glazes always have some silica and alumina within the kaolin or the clay, which makes the glaze hard, scratchproof, and highly resistent to acids. Since the glazes melt at the same temperature at which the body vitrifies, these pieces possess a relationship between glaze and body that is not present with low-temperature glazes.

Glaze Recipes

Cone 6a (1200°C/2162°F)

Potassium feldspar	40
Barium carbonate	20
Zinc oxide	12
Kaolin	10
Silica	10

Colemanite	8
Nepheline syenite	55
Dolomite	18
Barium carbonate	17
Zinc oxide	10

Cone 8 (1250°C/2282°F)

Potassium feldspar	65
Calcium carbonate	18
Kaolin	17

Potassium feldspar	35
Kaolin	30
Calcium carbonate	15
Silica	13
Titanium oxide	7

Potassium feldspar	46
Silica	34
Calcium carbonate	17
Kaolin	15

Potassium feldspar	46
Silica	26
Calcium carbonate	20
Kaolin	8

Bowl, 1997.
Thrown stoneware, 11 × 11 cm (4 3/8 × 4 3/8 in.).
Feldspathic glaze, 2% colemanite, zinc, and oxide.
Firing temperature: 1250°C (2282°F).

Menhir VI, 1984.
Hollowed-out stoneware with grog,
53.5 × 8.5 × 8 cm (21 × 3 3/8 × 3 1/8 in.).
Feldspathic glaze.
Firing temperature: 1280°C (2336°F).

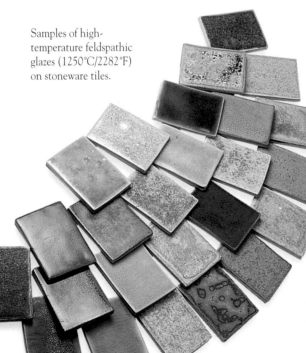

Samples of high-temperature feldspathic glazes (1250°C/2282°F) on stoneware tiles.

Sculpture, 1985.
Slab-built earthenware and grog body, 28 × 13 × 5.5 cm (11 × 5 1/8 × 2 1/4 in.).
Firing temperature: 1260°C (2300°F).

Very-High-Temperature Glazes

Mainly used for covering porcelain body, these glazes were used by potters in China as early as the Sung Dynasty (960–1279). Regardless of the technique used, these glazes are applied on ceramic bodies, such as porcelain, which vitrify at a higher temperature than stoneware bodies.

These clay bodies are mainly composed of kaolin, feldspar, and silica. A typical recipe for a body might be:

Kaolin _____ 50
(or bone China clay)
Feldspar _____ 25
Silica _____ 25

Silica can be reduced to 15 percent when the proportions of the other ingredients are increased.

The composition of these glazes is simple, just like stoneware. There is a close relationship between the clay body and the glaze, not surprising considering that they contain practically the same components.

These glazes produce very glossy, satiny, or matte surfaces. They are generally very resistent to acid, though not to hydrofluric acid, phosphoric acid, or the hot vapors of sulfuric acid. They have a low level of dilatation, making them very appropriate for ceramic mixes. They are also scratchproof and make for very durable pieces.

These bodies must be bisque-fired at about 1000°C (1802°F) and the glazes melt at 1200–1320°C (2162–2408°F), although hard porcelain body can reach 1400–1450°C (2552–2612°F).

Stone, 1986.
Reproduction from hollow-casting technique, porcelain body, 27 × 12.5 × 11.5 cm (10 5/8 × 5 × 4 5/8 in.).
Feldspathic glaze.
Firing temperature: 1280°C (2336°F).

Glaze Recipes

Cones 9–10 (1280–1300°C/ 2336–2342°F)

Potassium feldspar _____ 43
Kaolin _____ 25
Silica _____ 15
Calcium carbonate _____ 10
Zinc oxide _____ 4
Titanium bioxide _____ 3

Silica _____ 46
Potassium feldspar _____ 20
Calcium carbonate _____ 18
Talc _____ 16

Potassium feldspar _____ 45
Silica _____ 25
Calcium carbonate _____ 15
White clay _____ 10
Kaolin _____ 5

Rectangular Bowl, 1998.
Slab- and strip-built porcelain, 16 × 10.5 × 5 cm (6 1/4 × 4 1/4 × 2 in.).
Feldspathic glaze.
Firing temperature: 1280°C (2336°F).

Vase, 1998.
Slab- and strip-built porcelain, 46 × 31 × 9 cm (18 1/8 × 12 1/4 × 3 1/2 in.).
Feldspathic glaze.
Firing temperature: 1250°C (2282°F).

Trunk Vase, 1998.
Strip-built porcelain, 25 × 9 cm (9 7/8 × 3 1/2 in.).
Feldspathic glaze.
Firing temperature: 1280°C (2336°F).

CRYSTALLINE GLAZES

Crystalline glazes are those containing materials that make the glaze crystallize during the cooling period, such as zinc oxide and titanium oxide. Some crystals are microscopic; others are big enough to be seen with the naked eye. These materials give the glaze a shine, and the addition of oxides, such as cobalt, copper, and iron, give the crystals color. The most commonly used bodies with this glaze are stoneware, grog, and porcelain.

Crystalline glazes are fired like other types until maturation; the difference happens when the piece is cooling down. During the cooling period the temperature must be lowered abruptly, then the kiln kept at the lowered temperature for a specific period; it is then cooled again and maintained to produce the crystals in the glaze.

These glazes, which have a very low proportion of alumina, are applied in a thickness of 3–4 mm (1/8–5/32 in.). Because they are very watery, the piece should be placed on a stand in the kiln to contain the surplus glaze that drips off when it reaches its fusion point. The thickness of the layer itself and certain components can cause the glaze to crack or flake when it is dry, so it is advisable to add gum arabic to the mixture.

The temperature should be slightly below melting point, about 100°C (212°F), for testing out each case. It is highly recommended that you carry out some tests beforehand, to help maintain a steady and slow cooling time. The correct cycles and the right composition of glaze will produce a good crystallization. A digital pyrometer makes it much easier to control and maintain the temperature during a determined period.

The glazed pieces should be placed in the kiln immediately after glazing. Be sure to place them on alumina-covered support tiles before putting them into the kiln. If you touch the glaze, it can crack and flake, especially if you working with very big pieces, and retouching is always somewhat complicated matter.

Both the base of the piece and the support must be covered with a thick layer of alumina and water, so that they do not get stuck if the glaze drips or runs. If this does happen, remember that glaze is very fragile, so the

Plate, 1982.
Thrown stoneware, 5.5 × 35 cm
(2 1/4 × 13 3/4 in.).
Feldspathic glaze.
Firing temperature: 1250°C (2282°F).

Plate, 1982.
Thrown stoneware, 4.5 × 28 cm
(1 3/4 × 11 in.).
Feldspathic glaze.
Firing temperature: 1250°C (2282°F).

piece must separated with utmost care to prevent it from peeling or flaking. Polish the base with a sharp, fine-grain silica carbide stone, handling the piece with great care. Don't apply too much glaze to the bottom of the piece, because the glaze from the top will run down and compensate. Sometimes you may not need any glaze on the bottom.

Firing must be done in an oxidation atmosphere, so the electric kiln produces the best results, although a gas kiln will also work. The firing process is the same as that used for a high-temperature glaze, but on reaching 900–950°C (1652–1742°F), speed up the kiln until it reaches 1250°C (2282°F) in as short a time as possible to prevent running.

When the glaze has reached its melting point, lower the temperature quickly to 1180–1150°C (2156–2102°F) within 10–15 minutes, and then keep it within these limits for about two hours (depending on the capacity of the kiln).

After this period, lower the temperature again, this time to 1080–1050°C (1976–1922°F) within 10–15 minutes, then keep it there for two or more hours.

Allow the piece to cool down normally until it reaches room temperature. Once the kiln has been shut down, the process can be accelerated by opening the kiln's air vent or even by loosening the kiln door's fastenings without opening it.

The firing cycle can be complicated, so you should carry out several tests and note down the results, since each formula can vary and temperature maintenance may be different (varying from one to four hours). The cycles must be repeated because a rapid cooling of the piece impedes the production of crystals in the glaze.

Glaze Recipes

Cones 8–9 (1250–1280°C/2282–2336°F)

Potassium feldspar	46
Calcium carbonate	13
Kaolin	12
Colemanite	7
Lithium carbonate	11
Zinc oxide	11

Plate, 1982. Thrown stoneware, 4.5 × 27.5 cm (1 3/4 × 10 7/8 in.). Feldspathic glaze. Firing temperature: 1250°C (2282°F).

Firing graph indicating the firing of crystal glazes in an electric kiln measuring 50 × 50 × 40 cm (19 5/8 × 19 5/8 × 15 3/4 in.).

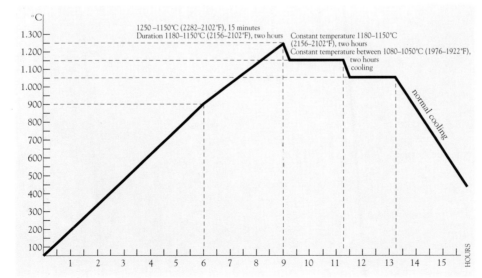

1250–1150°C (2282–2102°F), 15 minutes
Duration 1180–1150°C (2156–2102°F), two hours

Constant temperature 1180–1150°C (2156–2102°F), two hours
Constant temperature between 1080–1050°C (1976–1922°F), two hours
cooling

normal cooling

Potassium feldspar	46
Calcium carbonate	13
Kaolin	12
Colemanite	9
Titanium bioxide	10
Magnesium carbonate	10

Potassium feldspar	50
Silica	15
Zinc oxide	15
Kaolin	10
Titanium bioxide	10

RAKU

Developed in the second half of the sixteenth century, the raku ceramic technique is considered the essence of Japanese ceramics. It is used to make bowls and teapots used in the Japanese tea ceremony. These pieces have certain special color and textural characteristics that distinguish them from any other type of ceramic. They are made with clay bodies that can withstand very strong thermal shocks, and have a high percentage of stoneware (between 10 and 50 percent) and contain refractory clays and other materials used in the manufacture of high-temperature clay bodies. In addition to refractory and plastic clays and stoneware,

raku pieces may contain kaolin, feldspar, silica, and talc, among other types.

Refractory clays, such as stoneware and silica, make the ceramic mixture porous and together with talc withstand the thermal shock that is produced on removing the piece from the kiln and cooling it either by pouring water over it or by leaving it out in the open air. The body's resistance to fire is provided by the kaolin, feldspar, or silica. Plastic clays are generally very helpful for modeling.

Prepared properly, stoneware bodies can be used as well. If the clay body doesn't already have the right proportion of stoneware, it must be added.

You can also add 5 percent talc if you want the clay body to contract less.

Raku kilns do not need to be very big. They may be run by electricity, gas, coal, or firewood. A front-loading kiln is preferable because it is easier to remove the pieces than it is from a top-loading kiln. Both the base and the support tiles should be given a coating of alumina hydrate or a mix of 50 percent clay and kaolin.

There are two methods of making raku. In the first, known as the single-firing technique (see page 58), the piece is modeled by hand. The body is warmed near the kiln and is then glazed when dry. Next it is placed in the

Cup, 1998.
Slab- and strip-built stoneware with fine grog, 10.5 x 12 cm (4 1/4 × 4 3/4 in.).
Alkaline glaze.
Firing temperature: 950°C (1742°F).

kiln, which is almost at the glaze's melting point. Once it has melted, the piece is removed from the kiln with a pair of long iron tongs, 70–90 cm long (27 1/2 × 35 1/2 in.), and placed in a bowl of water or similar recipient with sawdust, newspaper, twigs, wood shavings, rags, or the like, and it is hermetically sealed. (The piece can

be half-covered in the recipient, to produce variations in color as well as cracking, metallic, or blackening effects.) These items burn up against the incandescent piece, producing a reduction firing (see page 53), which influences both the body and the glaze. Ten to fifteen minutes later, this process is interrupted by removing the piece and placing it in a bowl of water, which cools it down very fast. Submerging the piece in cold water (rapid cooling) makes the color stay the same as when it was removed from the recipient. It can also be left to air-dry (slow cooling), in which case certain oxides tend to reoxidize and the colors will be those expected in an oxidation firing.

In the second method, the piece is made with any of the

This raku ideogram can mean, joy, pleasure. freedom, happiness, or satisfaction.

Bowl I, 1998.
Slab- and strip-built stoneware with fine grog, 17.5 × 10 × 5.5 cm (7 × 4 × 2 1/4 in.)
Alkaline glaze.
Firing temperature: 950°C (1742°F).

Bowl II, 1998.
14.5 × 14 × 7 cm
(5 3/4 × 5 1/2 × 2 3/4 in.).
Slab-built fine grog.
Alkaline glaze.
Firing temperature: 950°C (1742°F).

Cup II, 1982.
15 × 10 cm (5 7/8 × 4 in.).
Slab- and strip-built
stoneware with fine grog.
Alkaline glaze.
Firing temperature: 950°C
(1742°F).

various hand-building techniques (pinching, coils, slabs, or strips), then it is thrown, bisque-fired, and glazed. Afterward it is placed in the kiln and fired at a standard melting temperature for glaze. After that point the process is the same as with the first method.

When the piece is removed from the kiln, it undergoes a very strong thermal shock, so the bodies must be prepared in a way that will withstand the abrupt change in temperature. Also the color has to be taken into account, since the glazes will be brought out after firing with white bodies.

Raku glazes are of the low-temperature type and can be prepared either with lead glazes or alkaline glazes. Since the body should be porous, the glazes tend to have low melting points, around 960°C (1730°F).

The glazes can be applied with any technique, although using the brush allows you better control over thickness and lets you glaze areas of the piece with different colors. The glaze may have 5–10 percent gum arabic when using the single-firing process, to keep it from sliding or crawling on suddenly entering the kiln. The bottom of the pieces should be left unglazed, to prevent melted glaze from spilling and sticking to the bats.

The coloring of the glazes is obtained through the corresponding metal oxides. Since this technique involves reduction firing, you can achieve reds with copper oxide and even lustrous colors such as gold from bismuth and silver from silver nitrate. The proportions of oxide colorings must be kept low to prevent the glaze from blackening during reduction. With practice you will get to know the time required for each glaze during reduction. Keep in mind that more time equals a more complete reduction. Thus copper oxide will redden during a prolonged reduction and turn green if it is too short or badly reduced.

Clay Body Recipes

Refractory clay (white)	45
Grog	35
Kaolin	15
Talc	5

Refractory clay (white)	60
Grog	20
Kaolin	10
Feldspar	5
Talc	5

Refractory clay (white)	34
Feldspar	25
Kaolin	25
Grog	10
Talc	5
Bentonite	1

Stoneware	65
Grog	30
Talc	5

Glaze recipes

800–900°C (1472–1652°F)

Borax	50
Colemanite	50

900°C (1652°F)

Colemenanite	80
Nepheline syenite	20

930–950°C (1706–1742°F)

Lead oxides (minimum)	70
Silica	25
Kaolin	5

Lead carbonate	50
Silica	25
Potassium feldspar	12
Calcium carbonate	8
White clay	5

Colemanite	65
Potassium feldspar	25
Lead carbonate	10

Lead oxide	50
Silica	30
Anhydrous borax	15
Kaolin	5

SALT GLAZES

During the sixteenth century, certain traditional pottery-making villages in the Rhine valley were using salt to produce transparent glazes, a technique completely unheard of before this time. The glaze was applied to rounded pots with a slim neck and a handle in the form of a lace. This glaze was also applied to glasses and jars, decorated with relief superimposed or stamped on top, which allowed the ceramic body to be seen. The texture resembled an orange skin. During that century and the next, the technique was perfected and quickly became widespread throughout Europe and North America.

The process of firing salt glazes is simple; it is the same as bisque firing, meaning that they are fired raw and dry in the kiln, although they can also be bisque-fired by raising the temperature to the body's maturing point, since it is necessary to reach this state in order to salt the piece. Next the piece is salted with common household salt, sodium chloride (NaCl), which is tipped in by way of two special ducts made for this purpose and installed next to the burners in the top of the kiln. The sodium chloride evaporates and combines with the silica clay, forming sodium silicate, a vitreous glaze, which is used to cover the piece. Dampened salt can be introduced into the kiln wrapped in

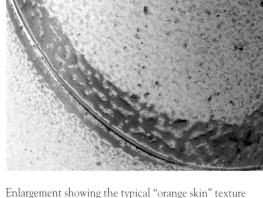

Enlargement showing the typical "orange skin" texture of salt glaze.

small paper bags or packets. The saltings are repeated until the glaze acquires the right thickness.

Salt-glazing kilns are used only for this particular method. Just as the salt glazes the piece, it also gradually covers the inside of the kiln. These kilns use gas, oil, coal, or wood-burning fuel. Although not very practical, the use of firewood as fuel produces interesting results in the glaze because the ashes mix with the saline vapors. Electric kilns should not be used for this technique because the saline glaze would damage the elements.

It is fairly easy to build a salt-glazing kiln. The bricks must have a low silica content and a high alumina content. You will need to make one or more holes for the introduction of the salt. The firing chamber must be checked each time you want to use it. All the shelves and supports used in the firing should be covered with a thick coat of alumina and water to prevent the glaze, and thus the pieces, from sticking to them. The door or the bricks that enclose the kiln must also be covered in alumina, as must the bases of the pieces for the same reason. Because the salt vapors must be able to circulate around the inside of the kiln, the pots must be placed at least 3 to 5 cm (1 1/8 x 2 in.) apart from one another. Unlike other high-temperature firings, lids must never be fired in place; they should be placed on stilts or spurs or on a tile that is also covered in alumina.

In this type of firing, pyrometric cones are of little use in indicating when the body has reached its maturing temperature since they become unusable once you introduce the first batch of salt. So you will have to examine the color of the flames to gauge the temperature. You can also use a pyrometer, but be sure not to place it in the kiln until after the saline vapors have disappeared, or

Bottle, 1984.
Thrown stoneware, 24.5 × 11 cm (9 3/4 × 4 3/8 in.).
Firing temperature: 1280°C (2336°F).

Bottle, 1980.
Thrown stoneware with incised decoration, 12 × 7 cm (4 3/4 × 2 3/4 in.).
Magnesium bioxide glaze.
Firing temperature: 1250°C (2282°F).

Plate, 1984.
Thrown stoneware, 4.5 × 27 cm
(1 3/4 × .0 5/8 in.).
Engobe decoration.
Firing temperature: 1280°C
(2336°F).

ventilation in the room where the kiln is placed. This type of kiln should ideally be placed outside, and covered accordingly.

The amount of salt to use should be proportional to the size of the kiln and the number of pieces you want to salt-glaze. Any hand-building or throwing technique can be used with the pieces you wish to salt-glaze.

Salt-glazed pieces are the colors of their clay bodies, al-

the pieces in subsequent firings, so it is more practical to apply the color to each piece.

The range of colors is limited by reduction firing (see page 53). Pieces can also be decorated with relief, texture, incising, or carving, which can be brought out with engobes and oxides, although the glaze itself will fill in these hollows and enhance the piece's volume.

This glazing method has a

part of the pyrometer will become glazed and, even worse, sealed at the opening through which it is inserted into the kiln.

The right temperature at which to add the salt depends on the type of clay being used. In general, stoneware is best suited to this process, so the temperature should be around 1200°C (2162°F). Once the salt has been added, seal the openings of the chimney for a few minutes to prevent the salt vapors from escaping. They can be opened up again once the smoke inside the kiln clears away.

Each addition of salt produces a temperature reduction of about 100°C. You will need to wait a while for the temperature to rise before you add more salt. It is a good idea to try out a few samples in the kiln to test the thickness of the glaze. Line up the samples in front of the peephole and then re-

move them with an iron rod. There should be at least one sample for each salting. Once you are happy with the glaze thickness, close the valves (in the case of a gas or oil kiln) or stop adding fire-

wood so that it can cool down normally.

The chlorine hydroxide vapors from the firing are poisonous, so you should have a chimney about 5–6 meters (16–20 feet) high and good

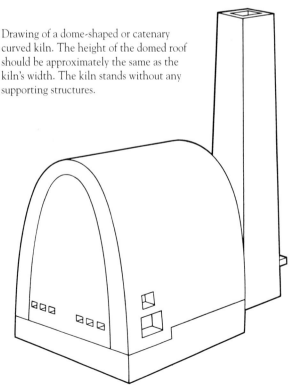

Drawing of a dome-shaped or catenary curved kiln. The height of the domed roof should be approximately the same as the kiln's width. The kiln stands without any supporting structures.

Plate, 1983.
Thrown stoneware, 3 × 21 cm
(1 1/8 × 8 1/8 in.).
Oxide colorings.
Firing temperature: 1280°C (2336°F).

though they can also be given another color. They can be decorated with engobes containing a high proportion of silica, colored with oxides. Or oxides with water can be applied to the raw or bisque-fired piece, which will produce a decoration similar to an undercoat. Cobalt oxides, copper, and magnesium are most commonly used for this process, but if you mix them with salt, they also adhere to the inside walls of the kiln, which can affect the color of

small drawback: the inside of narrow-necked pieces is not glazed by the saline vapors, so it necessary to glaze the interior before placing the piece in the kiln.

These glazes are very hard and resistant to acid and are nontoxic.

ASH GLAZES

Ash glazes began to be used in the East many centuries ago. It is thought they were accidentally discovered when certain pieces that were only meant to be bisque-fired became glazed when the ash rising from the combustion settled on the pieces and formed a glaze.

Obtaining ash for glazing requires a large quantity of burnt wood because about 90 percent of the material is lost during preparation. The alkaline portion of the ash dissolves in water; while other components, such as charcoal, are thrown away.

After burning the wood, the ashes are placed into a bucket of water and allowed to settle at the bottom, while the charcoal floats on the surface. The impurities should be removed and disposed of. The water should be changed several times until the alkaline substances are dissolved. The ashes are then sifted and put on a clean cloth placed on an absorbent surface, or in a cloth bag that is then hung up to dry. The ashes can also be used without washing them and are sifted dry in the open air or in a chamber with a ventilator fan.

Ash is a highly caustic material, so handle it with extreme care, making sure it does not fly up. Wear rubber gloves and, as when handling any powdered ceramic materials, protect your face with a mask.

Because of the high silica content, ash is not used in low-temperature glazes; 40 percent ash glazes are used at high temperatures. Ashes can be obtained from any type of wood, straw, reeds, nutshells, and other sources. The chemical composition is

Jar, 1998.
Slab-built medium grog
with additional decoration,
18×14 cm (7 1/8 × 5 1/2 in.).
Various ash glazes.
Firing temperature: 1250°C
(2282°F).

Samples of ashes: A. Redwood. B. Eucalyptus.
C. Fruit trees. D. Various.

quite varied, but there is always a high silica, alumina, and calcium content. Other elements such as potassium, sodium, magnesium, iron oxide, phosphorous, or magnesium may also be present. A chemical analysis of ashes reveals the content:

30–70 percent silica
10–15 percent alumina
15 percent potassium
30 percent lime

A typical recipe is as follows:
Ash _____ 40
Feldspar potassium _____ 40
Calcium carbonate _____ 20

Many types of ash melt at about 1260°C (2300°F), producing a liquid glaze. As always, it is necessary to carry out tests before using it to discover how the material behaves.

A glaze can be made from:

2 parts ash
2 parts feldspar
1 part clay

If the glaze is too liquid, more kaolin can be added, and if too hard, more ashes or other fluxes such as calcium carbonate. These materials are present in glazes in the following proportions:

Ash: 20–70 percent
Feldspar: 20–70 percent
Calcium carbonate: 5–20 percent
Silica: 15–25 percent
Clay: 5–20 percent

Other materials can be added, such as talc, titanium dioxide, colemanite, dolomite, or kaolin, as well as colorings such as oxides, although the natural colors produced by each type of ash are more interesting and genuine by far. Wood ash in a glaze in a proportion greater than 25 percent produces a very special result.

Bowl, 1998.
Slab-built medium grog with
additional decoration,
14 × 14 cm (5 1/2 × 5 1/2 in.).
Eucalyptus ash glaze.
Firing temperature: 1250°C
(2282°F).

Vase, 1998.
Slab-built medium grog with
additional decoration, 24 × 11 cm
(9 1/2 × 4 3/8 in.).
Eucalyptus ash glaze.
Firing temperature:
1250°C (2282°F).

Bottle. 1998.
27 × 10 cm
(10 5/8 × 4 in.) diameter.
Stoneware with
medium-grain
grog modeled with slabs
and additional decoration.
Ash glazes from fruit trees.
Firing temperature:
1.250 °C (2282°F).

Glaze Recipes

Cone 8
(1250°C/2282°F)
Feldspar	35
Wood ash	35
Kaolin	25
Clay	5
Nepheline syenite	40
Wood ash	40
Kaolin	10
Magnesium carbonate	5
Calcium carbonate	5
Feldspar	40
Wood ash	40
Kaolin	20
Nepheline syenite	45
Wood ash	40
Silica	5
Kaolin	5
Dolomite	5
Feldspar	35
Wood ash	35
Talc	10
Kaolin	10
Dolomite	6
Magnesia carbonate	4

CRACKLE GLAZES

Technically speaking, these glazes feature a defect, since the surface is covered in cracks, caused by a maladjustment between the clay and the glaze. Crackle glazes are produced by alkaline substances, such as sodium and potasium at low temperatures, or by feldspar clays at high temperatures, which have a high expansion rate. The numerous tiny cracks result from the different rates of contraction between the clay and the glaze. If, on the other hand, the glaze and the clay share the same expansion or contraction rate, the glaze does not crack. Crackle glazes are especially interesting when a particularly dense array of cracking is produced. These glazes can be transparent or opaque, glossy or matte.

To obtain this type of glaze, use a clay body with a low level of thermal expansion and apply a glaze with a high degree of expansion. Applying the glaze in a thick layer can also produce crackle. Another method is to add sodium and potassium to the glaze formula, since these encourage expansion, which will make the glaze crack. At the same time, the proportion of barium carbonate, calcium carbonate, and zinc oxide should be reduced. The increase in the proportion of alkaline materials in the glaze means the piece should be fired at the corresponding temperature, in order to obtain crackle glaze.

A rapid reduction in kiln temperature during the cooling process can also produce cracking in the glaze, as can removing the piece while still hot and submerging it in cold water or leaving it to cool down at room temperature. The temperature difference will cause the glaze to crack, but the formula of the clay body must be adjusted,

Bowl, 1984.
Thrown stoneware with incised decoration, 8.5 × 22 cm (3 3/8 × 8 5/8 in.).
Feldspathic glaze and iron oxide engobe.
Firing temperature: 1280°C (2336°F).

so the piece itself does not break. Cracking is typical in raku glazes, which are often cooled down very suddenly by removing them from the kiln and submerging them in a container of water, but in this case the body used to mold the pieces is prepared to withstand the thermal shock.

The very fine cracks of these glazes can be highlighted by applying color oxides, diluted in water. Another method is to wait for new cracks to appear and dye them with a different color, producing a contrast in the extremely fine crackle glaze. The piece can also be boiled in very saturated tea for about two hours; the color will penetrate the cracks and bring out the crackle motif. Inks and other colorings diluted with water can also be used to highlight cracks, but avoid using fat-based coloring substances because they are too thick to permeate the cracks properly.

These glazes are very appropriate for pieces made with high-temperature clays, such as stoneware and porcelain, and also with low-temperature bodies.

These glazes must never be used in ceramic pieces intended for food or beverages because the food or liquids will filter into the cracks.

Bottle, 1998.
Slab- and strip-built clay with medium grog, 28.5 × 21.5 × 8.5 cm (11 1/4 × 8 3/8 × 3 3/8 in.).
Alkaline glaze.
Firing temperature: 1000°C (1802°F)

Vase, 1998.
Slab- and strip-built medium grog, 27 × 18 × 7.5 cm (10 5/8 × 7 1/8 × 3 in.).
Alkaline glaze.
Firing temperature: 1000°C (1802°F)

Seated Figure (study), 1972.
Chunk-built thick grog, 31.5 × 15.5 × 16 cm (12 1/2 × 6 × 6 1/4 in.).
Alkaline glaze.
Firing temperature: 960°C (1730°F).

SCOTCH TOPAZ GLAZES

These glazes take their name from their similarity to a rock of the same name, a dark yellow quartz with fine layers of embedded golden mica. The earliest known glazes of this type originated in ancient China.

Scotch topaz glazes are transparent and shiny and are produced by a saturation of iron oxide with a very low alumina content. The glaze crystallizes on cooling, producing shiny reddish or golden brown crystals. The percentage of iron oxide ranges from 3 to 15 percent; the percentage is important because too much oxide turns the glaze opaque or cloudy. The flux may be lead, or alkaline materials such as sodium or potassium.

Firing should be at a suitable temperature to obtain a good fusion in an oxidation atmosphere, both at low and high temperatures, so an electric kiln is preferable. Pieces using this glaze must be cooled very carefully and slowly, under observation, especially during the crystallization of the iron oxide. As with crystalline glazes, these glazes may require several tests to discover the proper cooling time.

They can be applied over any kind of body, though the best results are obtained with iron clay and especially on bisque-fired pieces that have a coating of iron chromate.

This glaze should be applied thickly, about 3–4 mm (1/8–5/32 in.), otherwise the crystals will not form. The glaze runs easily, so place a container under the pieces to collect any excess glaze, or leave the area near the base unglazed.

Pot, 1998.
Thrown red clay, 15 × 18 cm 7/8 × 7 1/8 in.).
Alkaline glaze.
Firing temperature: 1060°C (1940°F)

Vase, 1998.
Slab-built fine-grain stoneware, 28 × 10 × 9 cm (11 × 4 × 3 1/2 in.).
Red glaze from copper.
Firing temperature: 1260°C (2300°F).

Glaze Recipes

Cone 02a (1060°C/1940°F)
Borax _____ 43
Feldspar _____ 20
Silica _____ 20
Lead carbonate _____ 12
Kaolin _____ 5

Cone 01a (1080°C/1976°F)
Lead oxide _____ 58
Sodium feldspar _____ 26
Silica _____ 13
Calcium carbonate _____ 3
Add 5 to 10% iron oxide to this formula.

Cone 8 (1250°C/2282°F)
Potassium feldspar _____ 40
Colemanite _____ 40
Silica _____ 20
Add 10–15% iron oxide to this formula.

Potassium feldspar _____ 40
Colemanite _____ 20
Kaolin _____ 20
Calcium carbonate ____ 10
Silica _____ 10

Bowl, 1998.
Slab-built stoneware with fine grog, 9 × 14 cm (3 1/2 × 5 1/2 in.).
Felspathic glaze.
Firing temperature: 1260°C (2300°F).

REDUCTION FIRING

A reduction atmosphere is one that burns with very little oxygen. It is produced in gas, oil, or wood-burning kilns by partially closing the air intake to prevent oxygen from entering the kiln. The principle behind reduction is relatively simple. When the fuel is burned, the carbon combines with the oxygen and produces carbon dioxide and heat. This carbon and carbon dioxide are highly active, especially at high temperatures, and attempt to combine with the oxygen inside the kiln. When none is available, they combine with the oxygen from the glazes, thereby affecting the color.

In this atmosphere there are two materials that release oxygen: ferric oxide (Fe_2O_3) and copper oxide (CuO). The first is reduced to ferrous oxide (FeO) while the second becomes cupric oxide (Cu_2O). In both reac-tions there is a reduction in the oxygen; in the case of iron from 3:2 to 1:1, and for copper from 1:1 to 1:2. This process produces a change in color.

In this atmosphere, the glaze colors are very different from those produced with the same formula fired in an oxidation atmosphere. Some glazes show a remarkable change in the surface, which becomes satiny and smooth to the touch.

The firing always begins with an oxidation atmosphere; reduction starts when the glazes are reaching their melting point, then firing continues again with an oxidation atmosphere.

Plate, 1998.
Incised medium grog with added relief,
17.5 × 17.5 × 17.5 cm
(7 × 7 × 7 in.).
Celadon glaze and porcelain engobe.
Firing temperature: 1250°C (2282°F).

Sculpture (maquette), 1983.
Slab-and slip-built fine grog,
14 × 13 × 13 cm
(5 1/2 × 5 1/8 × 5 1/8 in.).
Red glaze from copper.
Firing temperature:
1250°C (2282°F).

Electric kilns are not suitable for this type of firing unless they are equipped with a airtight box inside the kiln for holding the pieces. This box should have a direct outlet to the exterior, such as a small chimney, through which a reduction-producing material, such as naphthalene, can be introduced. Keep in mind, however, that reduction firing is not generally recommended with electric kilns since the reducing temperature corrodes the elements, thus shortening their life.

Plate, 1980.
Thrown grog, 4.5 × 20.5 cm (1 3/4 × 8 in.).
Metallic luster.
Firing temperature: 1000°C (1802°F).

CELADON GLAZES

These glazes, like many others, originated in China and were perfected during the Sung Dynasty (960–1279). They are feldspathic glazes that contain kaolin, calcium, and silica. They also may contain bone, vegetable and volcanic ash, dolomite, and talc. The iron oxide included in small percentages varies in color when fired in a reduction atmosphere (see page 53), producing shades of greenish, bluish or brownish gray, or olive green. The color changes according to the thickness of the glaze layer, and the length of the reduction and cooling periods. These colors can be easily

Plate, 1998.
Slab-built porcelain with sculpted relief,
7 × 27 cm (2 3/4 × 10 5/8 in.).
Feldspathic glaze.
Firing temperature: 1250°C (2282°F).

Bowl, 1982.
Thrown stoneware, 8 × 14 cm
(3 1/8 × 5 1/2 in.).
Firing temperature: 1280°C
(2336°F).

distinguished from the copper greens produced in an oxidation atmospheres. Firing temperatures are 1200–1280°C (2162–2336°F).

Celadon glazes call for a white clay with feldspar that vitrifies well, such as stoneware and porcelain. It should be applied in a thick coating.

This transparent glaze covers the clay and provides texture, penetrating into areas of relief and accentuating them through the different thicknesses of the glaze coating. It is also effective on smooth surfaces.

Celadon glazes can be made opaque with the addition of tin or zirconium oxide, although successful results may be difficult to obtain. Their color varies from gray to greenish gray.

When iron oxide is used in a proportion of 0.5–1 percent, a light green is produced. In proportions higher than 1 percent, a stronger green is obtained; 1.5 percent yields olive green, and 2 percent produces dark green. As the percentage is increased, the green becomes increasingly dark, until brownish tones are produced. At 7–10 percent, "iron reds" will result.

These glazes are reduced at about 800°C (1472°F) at the end of the firing process. The air and gas intake valves should be closed and the kiln allowed to cool down slowly.

Vase, 1998.
Slab-built porcelain with incised relief, 17 × 14 cm (6 3/4 × 5 1/2 in.).
Firing temperature: 1250°C (2282°F).

Bottle, 1998.
Strip-built porcelain, 27 × 12.5 × 11 cm (10 5/8 × 5 × 4 3/8 in.).
Firing temperature: 1250°C (2282°F).

Glaze Recipes

Cone 8 (1250°C/2282°F)

Feldspar	60
Silica	25
Calcium carbonate	10
White clay	5

Feldspar	34
Silica	30
Bone ash	17
White clay	15
Calcium carbonate	4

Feldspar	50
Silica	20
Calcium carbonate	17
Kaolin	3

Cone 9 (1280°C/2336°F)

Potassium feldspar	38
Silica	25
Calcium carbonate	13
Kaolin	11
Tricalcium phosphate	8
Magnesium carbonate	5

Silica	30
Potassium feldspar	27
Calcium carbonate	23
Kaolin	20

OXBLOOD GLAZES

In 1368, Hung Wu expelled the Mongols from China and founded the Ming Dynasty. During this period (1368–1644), Chinese ceramists produced extremely complex shapes and decorations and discovered red glazes, obtained through copper oxide fired in a reduction atmosphere (see page 53). These glazes are also known as copper reds and China reds.

Copper oxide, which produces shades of green in oxidation firing, produces reds in reduction firing, ranging from blood red to reddish brown, orange, vermilion, and even purple. The copper oxide changes from cupric oxide (CuO) to cuprous oxide (Cu_2O) and then to metallic copper (Cu), which is red. Above 1260°C (2300°F), copper begins to volatilize, and thus the red color may disappear from the glaze.

Oxblood glazes should be fired in an oxidation atmosphere until the glaze matures, then the atmosphere should be dramatically reduced while maintaining the same temperature. The duration of time will vary according to the kiln used. Various sample firings should be carried out to determine the exact time necessary. Keep in mind that these glazes are highly sensitive to heat, so it is difficult to achieve two firings with identical results.

The addition of 0.5–1.5 percent iron oxide to the glaze can provide good results. A transparent glaze can also be applied over the glaze, making the red stronger by preventing it from oxidizing again during cooling. Tin oxide added in proportions of 3 percent also helps bring out color.

Copper reds can also be produced in electric kilns and in an oxidation atmosphere by introducing into the glaze silicon carbide ground to 200- to 300-mesh fineness. This reduces the copper, removing its oxygen. The proportions used should be 0.1–4 percent because greater amounts may make the glaze bubble because of overly strong reduction.

The glaze should be applied in a thick coating, 2–3 mm (1/16–1/8 in.). Any glazing method will work, but because of the thickness gum arabic should be added to keep the glaze from crawling or sliding off the surface of a bisque-fired piece. For the same reason, the glaze has a tendency to drip off during firing, so a container or tray should be placed under the piece to catch any runoff. If the glaze is applied in precisely the right thickness and fired at the right temperature, and an area around the base is left unglazed, dripping should not occur.

This glaze should be applied to very white clays (stoneware and porcelain) that are compact, with very

Tray, 1998.
Slab- and strip-built stoneware with medium grog, 30 × 15 × 8 cm (11 7/8 × 5 7/8 × 3 1/8 in.).
Porcelain engobe.
Firing temperature: 1250°C (2282°F).

Vase, 1983.
Thrown stoneware, 20 × 16 cm (7 7/8 × 6 1/4 in.).
Firing temperature: 1250°C (2282°F).

little or no iron content. On pieces modeled with clay containing grog, an engobe of stoneware or porcelain should be applied.

Engobe Recipes

Stoneware
White clay ———————— 40
Potassium feldspar ——— 30
Kaolin———————————— 30

Porcelain
Kaolin———————————— 54
Potassium feldspar———— 26
Silica——————————————— 18
Bentonite ————————— 2

Glaze Recipes

REDUCTION ATMOSPHERE

Cone 03a (1040°C/1904°F)
Anhydrous borax ———— 27
Clay——————————————— 19
Lead oxide———————————— 15
Feldspar——————————————— 15
Silica————————————————— 14
Calcium carbonate ———— 7
Sodium carbonate ———— 2
Tin oxide ————————————— 1

Cone 02a (1060°C/1940°F)
Anhydrous borax ———— 25
Silica——————————————— 22
Feldspar——————————————— 15
Lead oxide———————————— 15
Calcium carbonate ———— 10
Sodium carbonate———— 5
Zinc oxide——————————— 4
Kaolin ———————————— 3
Tin oxide ————————————— 1

Bowl, 1998.
Strip-built stoneware with medium grog,
18.5 × 11 cm (7 3/8 × 4 3/8 in.).
Porcelain engobe.
Firing temperature: 1250°C (2282°F).

Bottle, 1998.
Slab- and strip-built porcelain,
33 × 17 × 12.5 cm (13 × 6 3/4 × 5 in.).
Firing temperature: 1250°C (2282°F).

Cone 8 (1250°C/2282°F)
Feldspar———————————— 46
Colemanite———————————— 18
Silica————————————————— 16
Barium carbonate ———— 11
Kaolin ————————————— 4
Chalk ———————————————— 3
Tin oxide ————————————— 2

Feldspar ————————————— 50
Silica ——————————————— 20
Calcium carbonate———— 15
Kaolin————————————————— 6
Zinc oxide———————————— 5
Tin oxide ————————————— 4

OXIDATION ATMOSPHERE

Cone 8 (1250°C/2282°F)
Feldspar ——————————— 40
Silica ———————————————— 30
Calcium carbonate —— 15
Kaolin ———————————— 10
Zinc oxide ————————— 3
Tin oxide ————————————— 1
Talc ———————————————— 1
Silicon carbide ———— 0.2

Feldspar ——————————— 53
Silica ———————————————— 27
Calcium carbonate———— 10
Colemanite————————————— 9
Tin oxide——————————————— 1
Silicon carbide ———— 0.8

SINGLE-FIRING

Long used in popular ceramics with good results, single-firing is still used today, although less often than the double-firing method. The single-firing technique entails firing a glazed ceramic piece only once. Raku and salt glaze utilize this type of firing, although some ceramists fire these pieces twice.

This method has the advantage of saving time and fuel or energy, since only one firing session is needed. It is thus the most economic method for making ceramic ware, as long as the results are satisfactory, in other words, if the proportion of broken or defective pieces is not too high.

Glazes applied to raw pieces integrate with the clay, producing extraordinary effects. Color and temperature parameters are the same as normal in the ceramic process.

There are some disadvantages, however. Since raw clay is more porous than bisque-fired clay, it is more difficult to make the glaze remain on the surface of the piece. The glazing system must therefore be adapted to each piece with more care than on bisque-fired pieces. Also, it is tricky to manipulate glazed raw pieces, which are much more fragile than glazed bisque-fired pieces, so it is harder to place them in the kiln.

Single-firing glazes can be fired at low, medium, or high temperature and adapt to any type of clay, but samples must be made to determine satisfactory results. These glazes should contain some clay to better adapt to the piece they will cover. Highly plastic types of clay are best. The glaze formulas should be precisely calculated so their shrinkage is the same as that of the clay they are covering. If not, the glaze may come away from the piece during the early stages of firing. Good results can be obtained with lead-based glazes.

Glaze can be applied both to dry pieces and to leather-hard ones. Any dust that may have gathered on a piece should be cleaned off before applying the glaze. Any glazing technique can be used, but each piece should be studied to decide which technique will be most appropriate. Because of the porosity of raw clay, these pieces require a thicker coating of glaze, since the clay may absorb some of the glaze during firing. But remember that dripping can occur with thick applications, so it is a good idea to wipe the base of the piece before firing. Also, to catch any dripping glaze, place it on a bat or above a receptacle that has been coated with alumina or a clay and kaolin solution. Another solution is to leave an area at the base of the piece free of glaze.

Because the piece absorbs the water in the glaze and becomes softer, it may collapse, so applying glaze can be a delicate task. It must be done carefully and quickly. Also, the moisture may produce cracks that may not be

These pieces were coated with lead sulfur (galena) glaze when they were in a leather-hard state. For the interior I used the pouring technique, and for the exterior I painted on the glaze in various layers while turning the piece on a wheel.

visible at first but show up after firing. If the glaze is applied on a leather-hard piece, the moisture already in the piece will make it more resistant to the moisture of the glaze, thus reducing the risk of breaks or cracks. There should be a high percentage of clay in the composition of this type of glaze.

Glazes used on bisque-fired pieces can be adapted to raw pieces by changing some of the components. These pieces should be completely dry before firing, and the firing cycle should be very slow, as if bisque-firing. After 600°C, the firing can continue as for a regular glaze firing.

The placement of the pieces in the kiln is the same as for a regular glaze firing. Keep them from touching one another so that the hot air can flow all around them.

On red earthenware clay covered in engobe, I have used the following formula with excellent results. The firing temperature should be 1040–1080°C (1904–1976°F), cones 03a–01a:

Litharge ———— 61
White clay ——— 20
Feldspar ———— 14
Silica ———— 5

I have also used the following recipe on stoneware clays with success. Be sure to test it before applying it directly on a piece. Firing temperature is 1250–1280°C (2282–2336°F), cones 8–9:

Feldspar ———— 36
Silica ———— 25
Chalk———— 18
Kaolin ———— 17
Bentonite ———— 4

Popular II, III, and V, 1974. Thrown red earthenware clay, II: 25.5 × 17 cm (10 × 6 3/4 in.); III: 18.5 × 12 cm (7 3/8 × 4 3/4 in.); V: 19 × 15 cm (7 1/2 × 5 7/8 in.). Lead-based glaze and engobe decoration. Firing temperature: 950°C (1742°F).

Song of Hope VII, 1994. Hollowed-out stoneware with medium grog, 26 × 14 × 9.5 cm (10 1/4 × 5 1/2 × 3 3/4 in.). Feldspathic glaze. Firing temperature: 1250°C (2282°F).

LUSTERS

Historically, to obtain lusters Arabic ceramists used alum with vinegar, cinnabar, iron oxide, and silver sulfur, among other materials.

Lusters can be produced in two different ways, either adding the ingredients to raw glaze, or applying them to a fritted one. The former technique is used with an alkaline or lead base. Various components are mixed in, such as bismuth subnitrate, silver nitrate, copper oxide, and copper sulfide. This is then fired in a reduction atmosphere (see page 53). These glazes produce iridescent colors due to their salt and metal oxide content, which reduce during firing so the metals become visible.

This process requires a very white clay body, such as white industrial earthenware clay. If you are working with red earthenware clay, cover

Detail of luster on red earthenware clay with engobe. Reduction atmosphere. Firing temperature: 1000°C (1802°F).

Vase I, 1985.
Thrown white industrial earthenware clay, 20× 13 cm (7 7/8 × 5 1/8 in.).
Firing temperature: 800°C (1472°F).

Vase I, 1985.
Thrown white industrial earthenware clay, 10.5 × 10 cm (4 1/4 × 4 in.).
Firing temperature: 800°C (1472°F).

it well with a white engobe when the piece reaches a leather-hard state. This engobe should have the same rate of expansion as the clay to prevent crazing, unless that effect is desired.

When applying a luster to a fritted glaze, the luster can be obtained from liquid preparations made of metal salts and oxides (bismuth, zinc, cobalt, copper, chrome, iron, silver, or lead, among others), which are then applied to a glazed and fired piece. The piece is fired again in an oxidation atmosphere, since the preparation contains a resin that acts as a reducing agent. During firing, the salts and oxides become fixed on the glaze, producing iridescent colors. This process can be considered a surface decoration.

The glazed pieces on which a luster is to be applied must be free of dust or grease, which would repel the luster. It should be ap-

Another detail of luster on red earthenware clay with engobe. Reduced atmosphere. Firing temperature: 1000°C (1802°F).

Engobe Recipe

White clay	50
Feldspar	30
Kaolin	20

Luster Glaze Recipes

Cones 07a–06a
(960–980°C/ (1730–1796°F)

Alkaline frit	100
Silver nitrate	2

Alkaline frit	100
Bismuth subnitrate	2

Alkaline frit	100
Copper oxide	3
Bismuth subnitrate	2

Cone 05a
(1000°C/1802°F)

Lead carbonate	58
Silica	24
Kaolin	10
Calcium carbonate	8

Lead carbonate	60
Silica	20
Feldspar	15
Kaolin	5

Silver nitrate, bismuth subnitrate, or copper oxide should be added to these formulas, either separately or mixed together. Lead carbonate has a tendency to darken in reduction firing.

Shape, 1997.
Slab-built white industrial earthenware clay, 37 x 13 × 10 cm (14 5/8 × 5 1/8 × 4 in.).
Firing temperature: 800°C (1472°F).

plied with a paintbrush, in very fine layers, covering part or all of the surface of the glazed piece. When dry, it should be fired in an oxidation atmosphere at a temperature lower than the maturing temperature of the glaze. In general, these firings are done at 800°C (1472°F) or even lower.

These materials, which dry quickly, should be stored in well-sealed jars to prevent their hardening, although they can be dissolved with turpentine or special solvents once dry.

Vase II, 1985.
Thrown white industrial earthenware clay,
15.5 × 11 cm (6 × 4 3/8 in.).
Firing temperature: 800°C (1472°F).

PREPARING FRITS

Frits

A frit is a mixture of materials that have been melted and cooled, then reduced to a powder. Found in some glazes, it makes alkaline materials insoluble (they are normally soluble in water), and lowers the toxicity of lead-based substances (lead carbonate). It thereby produces stable compounds that, together with other materials, produce glazes with highly controllable final results.

The components of frit are calculated, weighed, mixed, and placed in a crucible. The crucible is then placed in the kiln, with a receptacle containing water beneath it. When a certain temperature is reached, about 1000°C (1802°F), the mixture melts and falls into the water. The thermal shock due to the sudden cooling upon hitting the water causes the mix to fragment and break into little bits, thereby making the milling process easier.

Crucible

A crucible is a receptacle in the form of a truncated cone made of refractory material. It holds the materials that are to form the frit. Crucibles used in fritting kilns have a hole in their base, while those used in regular kilns do not, having a spout instead for pouring the frit out. The crucible should not be filled beyond two-thirds of its capacity, to keep it from overflowing during firing.

Each crucible should be used only for a specific type of frit, since part of the frit will remain stuck to the walls after each use. Crucibles with spouts should have their spouts blocked with a moistened bit of the material to be fritted.

If the frit does not flow out or the crucible hole is obstructed, an electricity-proof L-shaped wire (never a straight one) should be used to mix the frit until it flows out.

Fritting Kiln

A fritting kiln is almost identical to a regular kiln, powered either by electricity or gas. The only difference is that there is a hole in the base of the kiln. But a special fritting kiln is not necessary if you use it only occasionally. A regular kiln can be used, along with crucibles having spouts. They should be removed from the kiln with long metal tongs that can grip the crucible without it slipping. The liquid can then be poured into a bucket of water.

The other system, which is more practical, allows the melted frit to pour out through the holes of the crucible and kiln directly into a bucket of water placed beneath it. In both processes, the melted mixture will break into small pieces upon coming in contact with the water.

Ball Mill

The ball mill is used to grind the mixture into a powder, either fine or coarse, thus mixing the components. The frit can also be ground by hand in a mortar, but the ball mill produces a more homogenous mixture and saves time and energy. Powered by an electrical motor, the mill rotates the refractory or porcelain jars holding the frit or glaze. These hermetically sealed jars contain several dozen porcelain or silica balls, whose movement grinds the components of the glaze. The balls can be of varying sizes for better grinding, and, along with the materials to be ground and water, should occupy between 50 and 60 percent of the total capacity of the jar.

The glaze materials should be placed in the jar in a dry state. Water should then be added to approximately 50

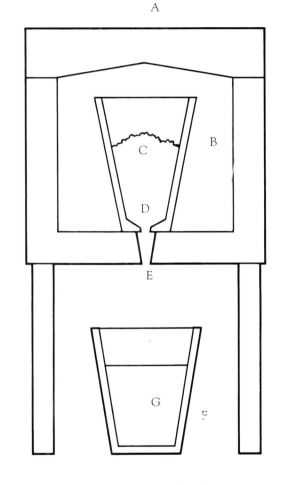

Cross-section of a fritting kiln with a loaded crucible inside. The melted frit falls through the holes in the base of the crucible and the kiln into the bucket of cold water.

A. Kiln
B. Crucible
C. Materials
D. Hole in the base of the crucible
E. Hole in the base of the kiln
F. Bucket
G. Water

percent of the weight of the materials. It is important to add the right amount of water, because if the glaze materials become too thick or too thin, they will not grind well.

The speed of rotation of the mill should be calculated. This can oscillate between 70 and 90 revolutions per minute (for small jars of up to 5 liters/quarts). The balls should fall continually from the upper part of the jar to grind the materials well. If the mill turns too fast, centrifugal force will keep the balls at the sides of the jar and the contents will not be ground. If the mill turns too slowly, the balls will remain in the bottom of the jar and will not manage to grind the contents either.

After milling, the contents should be emptied onto a wide-mesh sieve to catch the balls, which should then be cleaned carefully before returning them to the jars. Cleaning is especially important when changing colors to prevent coloring the new mixture. The balls will eventually wear out and will then need to be replaced.

The ball mill is used to mix ceramic materials in a dry or moist state: clays, oxides, and glazes, in addition to frits. It can also be used to mill the ingredients. It is powered by an electric motor that rotates two cylinders between which are placed hermetically sealed jars made of refractory material or porcelain.

GLOSSARY

Acids. In ceramics, materials such as silica and boric acid that form a fusible glaze when combined with metal oxides.

Alkali. Soluble salt that lowers the melting point of certain glazes.

Alum. Double alumina and potash sulfate. Used to prepare metallic lusters.

Anhydrous. Applied to bodies formed without the addition of water, or which have lost their water content.

Ash. Usually made from wood, straw, or the like. Used in some high-temperature glazes.

Atom. The smallest particle of an element. Atoms combine to form molecules.

Atomic weight (Aw). The relative weight of an element's atom as compared to the weight of an atom of hydrogen.

Bisque-fired. Ceramic pieces that have been fired only once and are not yet glazed.

Bisque-firing. Preliminary firing to harden ceramics prior to glazing.

Calcination. Process in which a ceramic mineral or mixture is fired at a certain temperature.

Carborundum (silicon carbide). A highly refractory and hard material. Used in the manufacture of bats and stilts in the kilns. It can be used in powdered form to add texture to glazes, as well as to obtain red colors from copper in an oxidation atmosphere.

Celadon. Glaze produced by iron oxide fired in reduction atmosphere at high temperatures. Its color ranges from green to greenish gray.

Chalk. Calcium carbonate (CO_3Ca).

Chemical compound. The chemical combination of two or more elements.

Chemical reaction. The combination of two or more substances, giving rise to a new one.

Cinnabar. Mineral composed of mercury and sulfur, very heavy and dark red in color. Formerly used to prepare luster.

Crazing; crackle. Cracks or fissures in a glazed surface due to the expansion and contraction of the clay and the glaze. Generally considered defects, but can be decorative.

Devitrification. When a substance changes from a vitreous to a crystalline state. Glaze can become partially devitrified during a slow cooling process.

Dipping. Glazing technique in which a piece is submerged in a receptacle containing glaze and then quickly removed.

Element. Chemical substance that cannot be divided into other, simpler substances.

Empirical formula. Formula for a glaze expressed in molecular proportions.

Firing. Heating of a clay object to a predetermined temperature.

Flecking. Defect in a glaze, in which flecks appear on the object's surface.

Formula. Expression of the chemicals combining to form a given substance.

Glaze samples. Small pieces of bisque-fired clay used to test a glaze before applying it to ceramic ware.

Hermetically sealed. Condition that does not allow air or fluids to pass through.

Iridescent. Showing or reflecting the colors of the rainbow. Shines and sparkles.

Leather-hard state. State in which clay is partially hardened but still retains a degree of moisture.

Lime. Calcium oxide.

Luster. A mixture of metal salts and resins that is applied to a glazed piece. The piece is them fired again at a lower temperature.

Matte glaze. Opaque glaze with a smooth texture.

Mixture. Union of two or more elements that do not form a compound. The elements can be separated again by physical processes.

Molecular weight (Mw). Sum of the atomic weights in the molecular formula of a compound.

Molecule. Smallest part of an element or compound that can exist in a free state.

Muffle. Chamber constructed inside a kiln that protects the pieces from the direct heat.

Opacifier. Material added to a glaze to render it opaque. Tin oxide is the best opacifier, but other oxides can be used as well.

Opalescent. Having the appearance or iridescence of an opal.

Oxide. Combination of an element with oxygen. Many of the materials used in pottery are oxides or combinations of oxides.

Oxidation firing. Firing in a kiln with ordinary atmosphere.

Paintbrushes. Used in glazing to apply the glaze and decorate the pieces.

Peephole. An opening in the kiln door for observing the state of the pyrometric cones inside as well as the color of the fire.

Pouring method. Method of applying glaze in which the glaze is poured onto a piece, usually a bisque-fired one.

Pyrometer. Instrument for measuring kiln temperature.

Recipe. A list of materials used in the preparation of a glaze, indicating the necessary quantities of each.

Reduction firing. Firing in which there is not enough oxygen to consume the carbon emanating from the glaze and the clay of the piece. This process uses up the oxygen, altering the color of some coloring oxides.

Refractory. Highly resistant to melting, able to withstand elevated temperatures.

Sediment. Material that falls out of solution and settles to the bottom of a liquid mixture because of its higher gravity.

Settling. Process in which a material falls out of solution to form sediment.

Sift. To pass a liquid, powder, or pulp through a sieve.

Silimanite. Highly refractory material used in kilns for its resistance to heat and high thermal conductivity.

Single-firing. Firing a raw clay object with the glaze in one firing.

Soluble. Capable of dissolving in water.

Spray booth. Equipment containing a ventilator or extractor and used to spray glaze on pieces.

Spraying method. Application of glaze with a spraygun and compressor.

Spraygun. Tool for spraying on glazes. Connected by a tube to a compressor, which produces the air to make it work.

Sprinkle. To spread a powder over a material.

Stacking. To load a kiln with raw and/or glazed pieces, distributing them evenly and efficiently so as not to block the hot air flow.

Stoneware. Glazed ceramic in which the clay and glaze have completely fused, producing a vitrified, nonporous piece. This results from firing at temperatures above 1200°C (2162°F).

Thermal expansion. Expansion of a material due to heat, and its contraction when cooled.

Toxic. Substance noxious to a peron's health.

Translucid. The characteristic of a body that allows light to pass, but does not allow objects to be seen clearly through it.

Turpentine extract. Viscous liquid that flows from pine trees and other trees; used as a solvent.

Vinegar. Liquid produced by the acid fermentation of wine; formerly used to make glazes.

Viscosity. Property of glazes that prevents them from sliding off the surface of a piece.

Whetstone. Special stone for sharpening and filing down objects.

White lead. Lead carbonate or ceruse.